a parent's guide for

raising *spiritually* mature teenagers

a parent's guide for

raising
spiritually
mature
teenagers

greg grimwood

Tate Publishing & *Enterprises*

Published by Tate Publishing & Enterprises, LLC
127 E. Trade Center Terrace | Mustang, Oklahoma 73064 USA
1.888.361.9473 | www.tatepublishing.com

Tate Publishing is committed to excellence in the publishing industry. The company reflects the philosophy established by the founders, based on Psalms 68:11,
"The Lord gave the word and great was the company of those who published it."

Book design copyright © 2007 by Tate Publishing, LLC. All rights reserved.
Cover design by Melanie Harr-Hughes
Interior design by Luke Southern

Published in the United States of America

ISBN: 978-1-60247-508-3
1. Christian Non-Fiction: Christian Living   2. Parenting

07.06.05

For Cara, of whom I am always sure.

Acknowledgments

Thank you, Father. When I take the time to notice your grace in my life, it renders me silent.

Thank you, Cara. When you're not around, I search the air for something. My cup overflows...

Thank you, my most precious Abigail Joy. Your first name means "Father's Joy," and that speaks everything. I look forward to our breakfast dates already.

Thank you, Mom and Dad. You are the best parents on earth. You convince me of this over and over.

Thank you, Nichole and Julie. Who could ask for better sisters? You two have always been pure joy to me. And Jewerl, I thank God that Julie has great taste.

Thank you to all of my grandparents, alive and in heaven. You shaped my parents beautifully, as they have shaped me. Gramps and Christine, you are saints to endure all of us on holidays!

Thanks to Morgan family for raising such a wonderful, godly woman in Cara, and for accepting me from day one. Molly, you've given Cara and me great practice for fifteen years down the road.

Thank you to everyone who supported me with your prayers and resources for writing this book. I could never repay you, even if I tried. I love you guys so much. Thanks for believing in me.

Thank you Rev Ron, for taking a chance with me. I wouldn't be in ministry today had you not stuck your neck out for me.

Thank you, Paula and Dave, for keeping me in the game, and for your friendship.

Thank you to my Valleyview Chapel family. Every last one of you is precious to me and my family, every last one. You are my taste of heaven on earth. Pete, you welcomed me with grace and open arms. I'll never forget you.

Thank you to my family at The Garage. Adults and students. We have something pretty cool between us. Matt and Lou, where would we be without you?

Thank you to all of my fellow leaders in ministry at Strongsville and Wadsworth. You've helped carry a heavy burden. I love doing battle with you.

Thank you to my beloved teenagers, all of you; you're the reason.

Thank you, Nygren, for never hesitating to have the pain-meter conversation with me.

Thank you, Grandma Thelma, for telling me that one day I should write a book.

Thanks, Joe, for being just like me in so many ways it's creepy. You were the reason I landed in Hillsdale. Thanks for being there from day one.

Thanks, Chap, for accepting me as I was and helping me become who I am.

Thanks, Bill, for teaching me about authenticity.

Thanks, Marcus, for teaching me about adventure.

Thanks to Dave and Dale. You've ruined me for Christ.

Thanks to the Christian men who have shaped my thoughts from a distance. I've listened to your teachings and read your books. Your fingerprints fill the pages of this book. Men like Dr. Howard Hendricks, Dennis McCallum, Gary DeLashmutt, Chuck Swindoll, Walt Henrichsen, and Andy Stanley...the list is large.

Contents

Introduction

Black-Belt Discipleship Moments

"Greg, there are some things we'd like to see you do differently."

I didn't hear much after that.

I was having coffee with two of my "all-star" teens from the student ministry, and they had decided that today was the day they would take over the youth group. They wanted more fun, more play time in youth group, less "serious stuff." They wanted to be entertained, and I was getting sick to my stomach.

You have to realize that by nature I am a people-pleaser. I don't enjoy people being upset with me, period; especially my two favorite teens from the youth group. However, today was different, no bones about it; they were presenting me with an ultimatum. They had the power to make or break our healthy youth group attendance and they knew it. They could double or cut the group in half in one week. Did I mention that I was getting sick to my stomach?

Their words seemed to float in the space between us, never quite connecting with me. The more they spoke, the more immense the gulf between us became. Someone once told me that there would come a time in my ministry years where I would have to decide if I was going to be a director or a leader. I never understood what he meant by that until that day in the coffee shop.

"I'm sorry, I need to interrupt." My voice was shaking, so were my hands. "I guess what I'm hearing you say is that you don't need me, you need a YMCA director. A game coordinator of sorts."

The boldness in my voice was shocking, even to me. They looked at each other, almost in a panic. The tide was turning and they could feel it. What happened from that point forward was nothing short of a personal revolution. I spoke with clarity, strength and unadulterated honesty. There were no apologies and no second-guessing. The decision was made, and the bluffing was over. I laid all my cards on the table and waited for some sign of life from the two of them.

Nothing.

"If we're through here, I have some work to do." That may have been my understatement of the year on so many levels.

They stood up, deflated and hurt, and walked with me to our cars. Before they left, I looked them eyeball to eyeball and said with truth and feeling something that neither of us will ever forget; it's something that someone once said to me.

"If I were to die tomorrow, and you two were to speak at my funeral in a few days, I think I'd want you to say that Greg expected more out of us. He expected us to be different."

One of them braved an understanding smile; the other just slammed the car door. And that is how it began.

Two years after "the conversation," I found myself on a stage in front of hundreds of people, reading the biography of the one who braved the smile. We met each other halfway across the stage. He presented me with a "life mentor" pin, and I presented him his Eagle Scout award. He braved the same smile and thanked me for having the courage to expect more.

I refer to that conversation a lot; it's the day that I realized that teenagers are literally dying inside for people to expect more out of them. I work with teenagers six days out of every week, and one thing that I see in them is an innate desire to have life-changing conversations, moments, and relationships. They are dying to be pushed and coached in something other than football, band, or academics. They are waiting for someone, somewhere to raise the bar for them in something that will live past their earthly lifespan.

Enter parents.

The Influence of a Parent

In the student ministry that I lead, one of our vision statements is "to partner with parents in the spiritual growth of their teenagers." I have a strong handle on the fact that I only have about a five percent rate of influence in the life of a teenager while their parents have a ninety-five percent rate of influence in their lives. In fact, if it weren't my current livelihood, I'd be the first and loudest advocate for less youth directors and more parent directors. Parents are grossly under-equipped when it comes to discipling their teenagers. This book will be my attempt at standing in that gap, drawing a line in the sand (insert favorite proper metaphor here). It's no secret that the most influential person in a young man's life is his father, and for a young woman, her mother.

As a youth director, I've talked with hundreds of parents. I've cried with them, celebrated with them, prayed with them, mourned with them, challenged them, and affirmed them. In my line of work, I've seen the best and worst of parenting. I've seen some parents raise tremendously mature and godly young adults, parents who were engaged with their teenagers in spiritual development. I've also seen parents who have either willfully or naively neglected this most important and honorable task of discipling their teenagers. They never had the difficult conversations. They never modeled a contagious and adventurous life in Christ. They never really wanted to know the dark and scary details of their teenagers' lives. These are the parents who I've cried with as their teenagers attempted to give life a go without God. A parent who is disengaged from their teenager's spiritual life almost always deals with feelings of regret and frustration.

I'm not writing this book from the top of some mountain. I'm writing this book as a youth director who has had a million conversations with parents. I've seen the differences in teenagers whose parents are involved in their spiritual development, and those whose parents simply choose to leave that part of child rearing up to the church. As a parent, you mustn't rely on a student ministry to raise your teenager. No matter how great the ministry, the influence is always limited. You must take a proactive approach; you must do the hard work of getting into your teenager's messy life and walking with them towards Christ. I'm writing this book from the perspective of someone who has "seen it all" in parenting, both the good and the bad. I'll share with you what I believe are the common characteristics and practices of those parents who have and are raising mature and godly teenagers; their methods are grounded in timeless Biblical principles.

If you are a single parent, take heart, this book is relevant for you. My suggestion is this: if you are *not* the dominant (same gender) parental role in your teenager's life, prayerfully decide who might serve as a good same-gender role model and ask them to read through this book with you, and both of you disciple your teenager in the same grace-oriented manner described in this book. It's important that your teenager has a positive and godly same-gender role model. Perhaps it's an uncle, grandpa, teacher, coach, family friend, or youth pastor. Anyone who already has a strong relationship and sense of trust with your son or daughter works just fine; my only suggestion is that they be Christian.

It's time for parents to step to the plate—we must. We can no longer sit back and allow our teenagers to get swept into the entropic drift of our society, which is taking them farther and farther away from God. If we aren't willing to take the lead of influence in our teenagers' lives, they will find someone or something else.

We've all heard horror stories about very godly people who have raised very rebellious children—children who stray and make horrible life decisions and then dutifully and beautifully find God on their own terms. Those are wonderful and touching stories of prodigal sons and daughters who have found their way back home, but I'm not convinced that those stories are necessary.

Obviously, each person chooses his own path and his own consequences, but I'm convinced that with gracious and godly guidance and support, we have a great shot at raising a young man or woman with a heart for God. Messy testimonies are great, but perhaps not as necessary as many of us think. For those of you who currently have a "prodigal" out there in the real world, please take heart. You can rest on these two pillars of our faith: 1. God is good. 2. God is in control. There is a chapter toward the end of the book specifically for your encouragement.

A Disclaimer

If your teenager is not interested in the things of God, *you must not force the methods of this book on him or her.* Parents are all too often guilty of forcing Christianity on their teenagers. This is very dangerous. If someone is not interested in the things of God, and we insist on continually shoving it down their throat or riding them in that area, it will push them farther and farther away from God.

The best thing you can do for someone who isn't interested in Christianity is to:

> 1. Spend a lot of time in your personal prayer time on their behalf.

> 2. Love them unconditionally and communicate that love to them in a way that speaks to them, not in a way that you feel most comfortable.

> 3. Accept them where they are; don't force them to act or behave in a certain way that *you* want if it's purely based on your personality. If he isn't a Christian, don't expect him to act like one. This isn't to say that you don't have and enforce rules, it just means that you should choose your battles very carefully.

Remember, Christianity is not about behavior modification, it's about a living relationship with God. Pray that they come to God as they are, and God will begin to change them internally. Don't focus on the externals! Love them into the Kingdom with grace and compassion.

I remember a tough situation during my second year in ministry. We were taking a group of teens on an overnight retreat that we had been planning for months. Our leaders knew that God had something special in mind for this weekend, and we didn't want anything to get in his way.

We were about to load up the vehicles when one of my key adults pulled me into my office with a look of concern and dropped the bombshell on me.

"I think Becky is high."

Becky (obviously not her real name) was a girl we had been trying to plug into the student ministry for a while. She had a pretty tough background and a lot of pain in her life. She was a sweet kid, and we knew that this weekend could be a real turning point for her.

"How do you know?" I asked.

"Well, unfortunately, it's pretty obvious. Do we send her home?"

"I hate to do that. Have her come into my office and I'll talk with her."

Becky walked into my office with her head down and her pupils dilated. Anyone who knew anything about the affect of drugs on one's body or personality could see that Becky was indeed high. I was disappointed and frustrated. We had a no-tolerance policy on drugs; if we caught a student under the influence or with drugs of any kind, it was a phone call to the parents and an immediate dismissal from our activity.

I happened to be reading a book called *Leading With the Heart*, written by my favorite basketball coach at the time, Coach K, and something that he said in the book kept coming to my mind as I was deciding what to do with Becky. "The truth is that many people set rules to keep from making decisions. Not me. I don't want to be a manager or a dictator. I want to be a leader—and leadership is ongoing, adjustable, flexible, and dynamic. As such, leaders have to maintain a certain amount of discretion."[1] Not every decision is a black and white decision; sometimes you have to go with your gut. Fair but not equal. Everyone gets treated fairly for their situation, but that doesn't mean everyone will be treated equally.

I finished the prayer under my breath and spoke. "Becky, do you want to go on this retreat?"

"Yes..." she said, sobbing, pleading.

"Then I'm going to put my neck on the line and let you come with us, but if you have anything in your pockets or bags, I suggest you make a trip to the bathroom to flush it down the toilet."

She grabbed her bags, went to the bathroom, then loaded into a vehicle.

That weekend, Becky received Christ. How stupid it would have been if we would have simply scolded her behavior without giving her an opportunity to meet Christ. What would have happened if at that point, I shoved Jesus down her throat and scolded her for "not acting like a Christian"? What would have happened if I tried to disciple her on why God doesn't want her using drugs? She wouldn't have understood. She didn't want to change, she wanted to smoke weed. Little did she know that when she became a Christian, God himself would make residence in her and give her a desire for holiness and disgust for drugs. That's what he does; he changes our paradigms. Until we have the Holy Spirit living in us, God's ways are foreign to us, we can't possibly understand them.

Don't force spiritual methods on someone who isn't a Christian, it won't take.

The Speed of Process

> When God wants to make an oak, He takes a hundred years, but when He wants to make a squash, He takes six months.
> —Dr. A.H. Strong

It's important that you understand on the front end of this thing that this process of discipling your teenager is just that, a process. This generation is spoiled with instant knowledge over powerful internet search engines, but knowledge is different than wisdom. Wisdom and godliness can only grow and develop with one four-letter word that you need to get a handle on in order to best make use of this tool: *time*. Significant and lasting spiritual growth happens at a very slow pace (the exception might be the initial kick-start of fast growth that God allows for a new believer). As a parent, you need to be patient with both yourself and your teenager. You're not going to read through this book and suddenly be "super parent," who spouts out life-changing and awe-inspiring godly wisdom while passing the mashed potatoes. If you do become that, you missed the point.

The truth is, this stuff takes time. Grace-centered discipleship isn't about instant gratification or behavior manipulation tricks. It's about the long, but steady, journey of walking beside someone toward maturity. This walk with your teenager will be awkward and clumsy at first, but lasting and eternal rewards await those who find the tenacity and perseverance to fight and pray through the awkwardness. You will eventually get to a place where the conversations and moments start to feel authentically natural and effective. It takes perseverance; the quality of a moment won't change by reading a book, it will change by leaning into God and moving forward with courage. Give yourself time. Give your teenager time. The growth is in the process. Trust me on this one.

Let's allow Proverbs 22:6 to give us some insight:

> Teach your kids to choose the right path, and
> when they are older, they will remain upon it.

The end of that statement is worth repeating, "...when they are older, they will remain upon it." Therein lays our goal. We are not interested in quick fix, instant gratification discipleship that leads our teens to momentary obedience simply because Mom and Dad said so. We are interested in preparing our teenagers for a lifelong love relationship with Christ. We don't want to bark commandments at them to stay on the path as long as they're under our roof; we want to compel them to live the rest of their lives on that path.

Sometimes Scary

Having authentic discipleship moments with your teenager involves getting intimately familiar with the fine-print details of your teenager's life. This can get sticky and sometimes a little uncomfortable.

Let me say it again.

This can get sticky and sometimes a little uncomfortable.

Now you have a difficult decision to make. The problem with discipling someone (especially your teenager) is that you have to really get into their life in order to "know" where the conversations need to go. I'm not talking about asking them about the easy stuff like school, track practice, and the latest friend gossip...I'm talking about the real and sometimes messy stuff. I'm talking about the things your teenager writes on his website, but hides from the dinner conversation. I'm talking about the dark struggles your daughter faces when she's alone with her thoughts or alone with her friends, the locker room discussion that your son contributed to after Friday night's big game. Do you really want to know what's going on in your teenager's head and life? Don't glaze past the question, you need to deal with it before you go any farther.

There is a price to discipling your teenager, and it begins with this question: Can you handle the reality of your teenager's life?

I've had more teenagers than I can count share with me some of the most intimate struggles they are facing in everyday life. Often times, when I ask them if they've shared this information with their parents, the answer is usually, "Greg, they couldn't handle what I'm telling you." Unfortunately, in many cases they are right.

Many parents suffer from something known as "ostrich syndrome." It's where we bury our heads in the sand and pretend that everything is right and wonderful in our teenager's lives. I'll ask the question again: Are you ready to take a genuine interest in what's happening in your teenager's life and head? As you engage in the process of discipling your teenager, expect things to come to surface that you never knew were there. Lean into God's grace and mercy and don't act shocked. Allow them to bury their tearstained cheek in your shoulders or beat your chest with their hands, but whatever you do, don't abandon them. Stand up and be the parent that God intended you to be.

My wife and I love Winnie the Pooh. We love his tender wisdom and deep friendships with Piglet, Tigger, and the rest of the gang. One of my favorite scenes in Pooh's life is when he's walking alone with Piglet through the forest...

Piglet sidled up to Pooh from behind.

"Pooh!" he whispered.

"Yes, Piglet?"

"Nothing," said Piglet, taking Pooh's paw, "I just wanted to be sure of you."[2]

Sometimes our teenagers just want to be sure of us. Let them know that you're there, you're with them, and you're not going anywhere.

My prayer for you is that this book will be a tool that you can use to take your relationship with your teenager to a place where you've always wanted it to be: somewhere deep and real, where you truly begin to understand and respect each other. Somewhere where you are able to gain back the elusive foothold of influence in your teenager's life and then steward that foothold wisely as you disciple them to become more like Christ. It's possible, and there's still time. If you're ready to get on with the story, I'll see you in the next chapter.

Grace-centered Discipleship

Last year, our student ministry started an outreach for teenagers who hang out in our downtown area. These are kids who don't want to go home, because to them, home isn't safe. From the very beginning, our team determined that we would profile for a certain type of kid. We designed and built the outreach specifically for those teenagers who didn't fit into a typical church youth group.

During one of our first weeks, we had a real scare. We were standing in the parking lot talking to a small group of people, when we saw one of our tougher teens walking angrily in our direction. He was looking for a fight, and it was with his ex-girlfriend, who happened to be in our little conversation circle.

In seconds, he was in her face ranting and raving and cussing and spitting. I looked nervously at the other leader standing with me. We both moved in on the situation before it got physical. I stepped into the space between them, making sure that if he cocked his arm back, I was in position to intercept the blow. Our other leader Matt, who spent some time in the army as an MP, immediately began to "talk him down." In other words, he very calmly but very firmly took control of the situation, deflating the hot air that was quickly escalating to fire.

That hasn't been our only close call. We have runaways, drug users, kids being abused, abusers, fifteen-year-olds with felonies, dropouts, ex gang members...you name it, we've got it. A lot of people are surprised, even shocked by how much we allow these kids to get away with. Our only rules at The Garage are: 1) Respect other people. 2) Respect other people's stuff. So we have teenagers smoking cigarettes, we have teenagers who cuss and litter and do all sorts of messy and unsettling things. To be frank, it makes the staff a little uncomfortable from time to time, but we determined from the beginning that The Garage would be a place where, perhaps for the first time in their lives, these kids would experience what grace feels like.

Sometimes churches and ministries turn into "behavior management programs" rather than focusing on introducing people to a life-changing relationship with Jesus Christ. What would happen if we gave a list of rules and regulations to every kid that came to The Garage. We could have a pretty long and detailed list:

- Don't cuss.
- Don't be mean to each other.
- Don't throw the basketball across the street when you miss a shot.
- Don't litter.
- Don't wear T-shirts that contain bad messages.
- Don't have green hair.
- Don't have more than seventeen visible piercings.
- Don't make fun of the youth director for being bald.

Okay, so maybe that last one is reasonable, but having such a list would be absolutely counter-productive. In case you've never had failure in this area of life experience, let me save you the trouble: *giving teens a list of rules and regulations doesn't draw them closer to Jesus Christ.* Drawing teens to Jesus Christ is exactly what we're trying to do.

Let's unpack this concept by looking at Paul's struggle between keeping a list of rules, the law, rather than focusing on his position in Christ:

> I don't understand my own actions. For I do not do what I want, but I do the very thing I hate. Now if I do what I do not want, I agree with the law, that it is good. So now it is no longer I who do it, but sin that dwells within me. For I know that nothing good dwells in me, that is, in my flesh. For I have the desire to do what is right, but not the ability to carry it out. For I do not do the good I want, but the evil I do not want is what I keep on doing. Now if I do what I do not want, it is no longer I who do it, but sin that dwells within me. So I find it to be a law that when I want to do right, evil lies close at hand.
>
> Romans 7:15–21

Paul is speaking of a struggle that most of us face as Christians. We all nod our heads in agreement every Sunday morning as the pastor teaches about holiness and the importance of avoiding those things that might pollute our hearts, such as lust, jealousy, or anything that keeps us from loving God and others more than ourselves. We've all sat around the bonfire singing "Kum Ba Yah" and filling out pieces of paper with our sins of choice, then nailing them to some wooden cross or throwing the paper in a bonfire, promising God that we will never do that again. Sometimes it lasts...for a week. Then we find ourselves doing the same sin, beating ourselves up all over again, and resigning to the fact that it's just something we will never overcome. That's a real shame; that's not how God intended it to happen.

Think of it this way, if you tell a child not to eat a cookie out of the cookie jar, what will be the end result? He will find a way to eat a cookie out of the cookie jar, even if he's a good kid. You've already planted the thought in his head by telling him what not to do.

Think of something closer to home. What besetting sin in your life seems to be impossible to "give up"? What is it that you have vowed a thousand times to God that you will stop doing? I don't mean to sound like Dr. Phil, but how is that approach working for you? The problem is, you're trying so hard to not sin that you inevitably do what you're trying not to do by sheer force of focused attention. Even if you're trying not to do something, by merely thinking about not doing it you are sabotaging yourself, because any active thought turns into action sooner or later. The very thing you don't want to do, you do. Then you get frustrated and beat yourself up, just like Paul did ("Oh, what a miserable person I am" (v.24)), just like your teenager does.

This is a dangerous downward spiral, which unfortunately leads to many teenagers measuring their "level" of Christianity by mentally keeping track of how often they sin. So Billy Bob goes to bed at night, mentally counting how many times he cussed today. If he only cussed twice, and one was something he considered a minor cuss word, he feels okay about his relationship with God and prays. On the other hand, perhaps he got hit in the head with the basketball during gym class and dropped a couple "f-bombs," he skips right on past his evening prayers, not feeling worthy of the God who loves him more than he has been conditioned to believe.

It's the same principle that parents should use when discipling their teenagers. Discipling your teenager is not about giving them a list of all the rules and imperatives of Christianity before they even have a handle on their new identity, let alone the practical and eternal benefits of their new standing with Christ. It's your job to help them discover for themselves who they are in Christ and what implications that has for their lives. It's about helping them tap into the infinite resources of love, power, and transformation that God has freely given every believer through our relationship with him. The results will be dramatic and invigorating. Once someone has a real grasp on their identity in Christ, they will experience a freedom and grace that compels them toward growth. They will find hidden resolve to overcome besetting sins, as well as experience a fuller joy and peace in their walk with Christ. It's the difference between spiritual growth through law and spiritual growth through grace. In this book, we'll call the latter form of growth "grace-centered discipleship." Quite simply, grace-centered discipleship means that we will partner with God in compelling our teens toward a deep and rich relationship with Christ by teaching, modeling, and praying that they would come to a full understanding of the depth of love and truth found in Christ.

When parents mistakenly see spiritual growth as sin management rather than grace-centered growth in Christ, the results can be devastating for their teenagers. They go through junior high and high school as seemingly godly, respectful, "by the book" teenagers. Unfortunately, as they go off to college, they realize that they don't even have a relationship with God, they have a relationship with rules; rules they will gladly toss aside for a season. Eventually, they become disheartened and quit trying.

They have been conditioned to try to live according to a set of rules under their own willpower, only to discover that they just don't have the strength. Another danger is that teenagers in this situation tend to think that they only answer to their parents, and when their parents aren't around to "police" their actions, they have the freedom to act however their impulses direct them. That's why it's important for parents to help their teenagers transition to ultimately being responsible to God, rather than parents or their youth directors. Our teenagers need to understand that it's even more important to do the right thing when nobody is looking.

Forcing someone to obey Christian commandments without the backdrop of nurturing a personal relationship with Christ and helping them understand their identity in Christ is like having a father who abandoned you at birth, and then one day shows up at your doorstep with a list of rules that he wants you to obey. There just wouldn't be a lot of motivation to obey. In fact, there would be motivation to rebel, which is where a lot of teenagers are with God. They see him as the dad they don't even know, showing up at their doorstep with a list of rules.

A Better Way

Many of us have been raised with the concept of sin-avoidance as the only means to spiritual growth; we knew of no other way. The grace of God sounds like a really powerful concept, but also really heady and philosophical. How do we put meat on the concept? What does it look like in daily, practical terms? Let's take a closer look at what this grace-centered approach looks like.

Let's first contrast the two methods of growth to give you a better distinction. The first and, unfortunately, most popular method used in most discipleship programs today is also the least effective. This method majors on focusing someone's attention on the law or a list of rules to keep. It is terribly ineffective for reasons we've already talked about. The other discipleship method, which takes longer but has much richer and longer-lasting results, is all about helping your teenager grow under grace by helping them understanding their identity and position in Christ.[3] I believe this is the path of spiritual development that God intended for us to experience.

Dennis McCallum, in his book, *Walking In Victory*, provides a wonderful chart contrasting the two methods of spiritual growth. It's a chart worth studying before you go any farther. As you're studying this chart, take note of some of the areas with which you struggle. Where are you living under the law? Where are you putting your teenager under the law? How will this information better help you to experience the life-changing grace of God? How can you share God's grace with your teenager? What perspective in yourself do you need to challenge? In your teenager? Spend some time with this chart; it could have significant implications for your intimacy and fulfillment in Christ, as well as that of your teenager's.

Area	Under Law	Under Grace
View of the Law	A set of detailed obligations that I must keep.	The underlying principles of the law describe the ultimate goal toward which God is moving me: a loving lifestyle.
View of self	I am regenerate, and therefore I am able to keep the law.	I am regenerate, but I still can't keep the law on my own because of my sin-nature.
View of others	A threat to your feelings of acceptance if they are more righteous than you. An excuse for self-righteousness if they are less righteous than you.	Means of receiving God's love and opportunities to give God's love.
View of the Holy Spirit	Little practical understanding of the Spirit's ministries.	Depends on the Holy Spirit for all power, motivation, and direction.
The "key" to spiritual growth.	Moral willpower *or* Special experiences	Knows self-effort is futile (ROM 7:18). By relying on the Spirit, not the letter, I can gradually change. Looks to a process, not to quick-fix experiences.
View of the "Means of Growth"	Ways to keep or get God's blessing	Avenues through which we expose ourselves to the life-changing power of God
Mental focus	What do the rules require? What am I *not* allowed to do?	My new identity in Christ. My personal love-trust relationship with God. Loving others as a means of growth.

Motivation	Fear/threat and guilt. What will God or others do to me if I sin?	Grateful response to God's love and grace.
Reaction to Trials	View as God's punishment; suspicious of God's retribution.	Confident of God's loving discipline.
Reaction to spiritual failure	Surprised and distressed. Rationalizations, minimization, blame-shifting, and self-recrimination. Vows to do better.	Not surprised. Confident of God's acceptance & therefore can admit sins to self & others. Responds well to admonition. Repentance & return to active dependence.
Reaction to spiritual success	Proud and intolerant of others.	Humbly grateful. Still able to empathize with those who fail. Sees continued need for growth.
Long-term result	External, superficial conformity, but increasing internal defeat and hypocrisy which leads to: Growing cynicism & giving up *or* Self-righteous externalistic comparisons—self-deception	Gradual transformation into a person who remains focused on his identity in Christ, with an increasing measure of victory over sin. A more loving, other-centered person.

(Dennis McCallum, Xenos.org)

Again, I encourage you to spend a lot of time reflecting and praying through this chart. Just being aware of the differences between the two methods puts you way ahead of the curve.

Helping teenagers grow spiritually through a grace-centered approach is best accomplished by educating them in two specific areas:

1. Their new identity in Christ.

2. What role they play in their spiritual growth, and what role the Holy Spirit plays.

All too often, we try to do the heavy lifting of spiritual growth that God never intended us to handle alone; that's why he sent us a "helper," as Jesus referred to the Holy Spirit.

In the next chapter, we'll look at what it means to help your teenager understand her identity in Christ.

Who's Your Daddy?

I love what Stewart Briscoe said about our identity in Christ, "If we spent more time telling people who they were in Christ, we could spend less time telling them how to act." We bombard our teenagers with rules on what is and what isn't acceptable for them to do as a Christian, and then we wonder why they hate reading the Bible and hate going to youth group. If we're doing this whole discipleship thing correctly, we are simply helping them recognize where God is urging them to change through convictions. Then we simply help them follow through with their own personal convictions. We mistakenly think that we have the capacity to change someone's heart and desires, when that is God's job. I'm not insisting that we don't bring certain things to light in their lives that are obviously against God's will. I'm simply suggesting that most of the time, people already know; we're simply there to encourage them to stop kidding themselves by pretending it's not a problem and to take action on their convictions.

It begins with helping them to understand their new identity in Christ. Imagine something with me; transport yourself back to another place and another time. Let's say you are a peasant. You labor and toil all day long, you work the land. Yours is a life of not much promise; things probably won't ever change for your. If you're a big dreamer, there's not a whole lot of hope for fulfilling your dreams outside of being a peasant. Your dad was a peasant, so was his dad....and your sons and their sons will be peasants too. Then one day you get a letter. You were accidentally switched at birth in the local hospital. You find out that you are actually the son of a king (I know, I know, it's a less than perfect example, but forget about the emotional scars that would come with such a situation and stay with me). You are immediately escorted from the fields to the castle. You are given royal clothing and awesome responsibility. You are given the choicest of foods and have the wealth of an entire kingdom at your fingertips.

Do you think you would feel differently about yourself?

Would you think differently?

Would you act differently?

The thing is, most Christians have never come to terms with the fact that their Father is a King. They're still acting as though they never changed, but they have. We are all new creations once we surrender our lives to Christ; he literally changes our identity. If we can spend more time convincing the peasants around us that they are kings, we can spend less time convincing peasants to act like kings. Once they understand their new identity, the changes in their actions and attitudes will develop naturally and swiftly.

This change of paradigm in understanding who you are, who God is, and who you are when God welds you together with him can be a dramatic experience. Dramatic for believers in that they finally begin to understand the depths of grace that God shares with us. Dramatic for nonbelievers because once they realize who God is, they can't possibly live another minute without him.

My little sister almost wore out our family's knees. We all had spent hours in prayer for her as she was going through a stage of rebellion in college, and we weren't very confident of her eternal address. One day, as I was about to drive back to my apartment after visiting with my parents,

I had a gut check. Something deep inside of me was telling me to go up to my sister's old bedroom where she was hanging out and have a heart-to-heart with her. Frankly, I was hesitant to have the conversation because I was tired and wanted to get home. I also knew that what I had to say could open up a can of worms, leading to yet another long and painful conversation, but it was clear to me that this was something important for me to do, so I followed God's prompting.

I found Julie on her bed. I don't remember if she was reading or watching TV or what, but she was up for a talk.

"Julie, can I just shoot it straight with you?"

"Sure, Greg, shoot away."

"I think God wants me to make sure that you're clear about one thing."

Oh, brother, she said with her eyes.

"No, seriously, you need to hear this."

She looked at me in the eye, as if to say, *This is your chance. Say what you need to say and then let me be.*

"Julie, I think God wants me to tell you that if you knew how much he loved you...I mean if you *really* knew...you'd stop running from him. You have no clue, no idea, no concept of how deep and wide his love for you is. That's all. He loves you...he loves you."

Her hard eyes began to soften and dampen. She looked back down at whatever she was doing, but this time with less interest in the book or television and more interest in what I had just said. It had affected her; God was working on her heart in a very real way, and it was time for me to go.

"I love you too, Julie, and I'll talk with you later, okay buddy?"

Two weeks later, I came home from church and there was a message from my dad on the answering machine. I'll never forget it; in fact, I could live off the high it induced for the rest of my life.

"Greg! This is Dad. We're having a party at the Grimwood household today! Julie received Christ at church!"

It's funny, I don't know how many times I've told that story, but the emotions are just as raw as the day it happened. That's what God's grace looks like. It's not hard, steely rules; it's a personal relationship with the God of the universe. It's like a peasant making friends with a king, and *that*, my friends, is what we want our teens to discover.

Since that time, Julie has grown in her walk with Christ by leaps and bounds and has married a very godly man. It's amazing the natural and lasting transformational effect that happens when someone truly gets a grip on what God thinks about them and how God sees them.

Our actions flow out of our identity, as does our sense of security. To explore this concept further, let's take a look at some of the unhealthy, but common, identities that teenagers adopt for their own lives.

Identity Based on Relationship with Boyfriend

Many teenagers, and I believe this is especially true with teen girls, have an emotional vacuum in their hearts. They cling onto another teenager in a way that they feel is filling the emptiness. Unfortunately, the emptiness they are experiencing is a direct result of an anemic relationship with their parents. With girls especially, it is very important that the father takes a proactive and loving approach in developing strong bonds with his daughter. Teenagers who don't have that connection tend to search for acceptance, meaning, security, and "love" from a fifteen-year-old in the form of a dating relationship. They build their whole lives around this relationship. They schedule their classes so that they can walk through the halls together. They spend significant time with each others families, splitting the holidays as if they were already married. They buy the same cell-phone plans with free texting. Pretty soon, their whole world revolves around this horribly dysfunctional relationship. Then one day, the inevitable happens. He breaks up with her, and her life is ruined. Life falls apart around her because he was the glue holding her world together. She goes anywhere and everywhere she can to find validation. If only someone would have walked beside her and pointed her in the direction of her heavenly Father, she could have met the one who knows everything that she's ever done and loves her still. She could have experienced relentless acceptance and eternal love. She could have filled her vacuum with the real thing. A sometimes unfortunate sidenote to this is that most teenagers will view their heavenly Father through the filter of how they see and what they think about their earthly father. For some teens this is a good thing, for others it's devastating.

Identity Based on a Sport

Identity based on a sport is a bit tricky. There are some very valuable characteristics that can be developed in a young person's life through sports, and I'm a huge fan of teenagers playing sports, but you have to be careful. It can't consume you, and you can't allow it to consume your teenager. When it consumes your teenager and they start to feel that the sport is their identity, it becomes very dangerous. They need to know that you love them for them, not for what they can do on the football field. I played basketball and experienced a lot of success, but I never felt that my parents only loved me or admired me or respected me because I played basketball. They loved me unconditionally and made sure that I knew it. Those long nights in the gym working out with Pops taught me about hard work, discipline, consistency, and many other characteristics that have shaped the man that I am today. My mom talked with me about other things that I was interested in as well, like art and reading and the value of being well rounded. Both of them taught me immensely and loved me unconditionally. Make sure you do the same for your teenager. Here is what an unhealthy relationship between your teenager and sports might look like (I'll use basketball as the example, since that's the sport I know best).

He spends hours and hours outside shooting hoops. If there's a gym open, he's there. If there's a pick-up game, he's the first one picked. If there aren't any hoops available, he's doing ball-handling drills, dribbling exercises, lifting weights, jumping rope, running, sprinting, jumping. He's always searching for the newest trend, the next big piece of exercise equipment that will take his game to the next level. His summer is packed full with camps and leagues and tournaments and games and drills. He doesn't have time for friends. He hardly ever eats dinner with the family. His dad talks nonstop to friends and coworkers about his son's latest stats and accomplishments. All the while, his son listens and solidifies in his own mind the fact that Dad sees him as a basketball player, so that's how he sees himself. His life is wrapped around an orange leather ball.

One day he graduates from college and realizes that his identity is being ripped away from him. All those years of organized ball, and now...nothing. He gets a job, but his real life is wrapped up in the three YMCA leagues that he's playing in, or the basketball channel that has twelve-hours-a-day live basketball action, both college and NBA. He convinced his buddies to join his fantasy league, and their draft party will be next Sunday afternoon, right after the Gus Macker 3-on-3 championship game. He still re-hashes the "glory days" every time he gets together with his buddies, and he's kept the old trophy room just as clean as it was the day he moved his son's room to the basement. I have a friend who attended his twenty-year high school reunion a couple years ago, and he said something that I thought was very interesting. He said that the jocks were still the jocks, the preps were still the preps, the brains were still the brains...everyone was exactly the same, they just had older skin. What a shame that after twenty years, the only thing the high school quarterback could think of talking about was the Hail Mary pass he sent to the end zone the final game of the year...twenty years ago. Nothing could be more pitiful.

Identity Based on Unfair Expectations from Parents

This is going to be painful, this might hit home, so brace yourselves. Some of you are living vicariously through your teenager. Stay with me on this. If you aren't supportive of something your teenager is involved in simply because you can't see yourself doing it, that's a problem. That's not fair to your teenager. If you've always wanted your son to play football, but he decides instead to be a cross-country runner, then you need to check your personal ambitions at the door and be the most supportive cross-country parent in town. If you've always wanted your daughter to go to Harvard, but she works hard at barely maintaining a 3.0 GPA, you need to be supportive of her work ethic and not make her feel unworthy of your approval by measuring her grades against an unfair standard in your own mind. Parents, it's time for some of us to get over ourselves and spend that energy working on supporting our teens in areas where *they* feel passionate and called. Our job isn't to make them into "mini-mes" when it comes to interests and vocation; our job is to make them into "mini-mes" in the area of character and godliness. If a teenager feels like she's never meeting her parent's approval because she isn't living up to "Dad's dream for my life," she will never fully experience the unconditional love and security of God, which should be modeled by her parents.

There is a fine line between having a healthy level of high expectations for your teen and living vicariously through them. I'm all about raising the bar for your teenager; in fact, we'll spend time on this subject later in the book, but living vicariously through your teenager is dangerous because you are forcing your own agenda in areas where they should have freedom to make their own decisions. When it comes to hobbies, sports, and other interests, your job as a parent is to help them discover what *they* love to do and then be their loudest cheerleader.

I remember when my wife decided that she was going to become a Mary Kay beauty consultant. I was pretty unsupportive at first. In fact, I made it known to her that this was not something I approved. As I prayed and thought about it, I realized that it's not about my desires for her; it's about her finding a place where she feels she can thrive in life and in ministry. My first Mary Kay convention was very interesting. The room was packed full of thousands of Mary Kay ladies. It was bizarre. There were maybe five other guys in the whole arena. When my wife was called up front to walk across the stage, I worked my way up to the very front row. I decided that if I was the only person in that room who was going to give her a standing ovation, she was getting a standing ovation. Fortunately, I wasn't the only one. The point is, you need to go out of your way to be the biggest supporter, the loudest cheerleader for your teenager's dreams. Remember, it's their passions and giftings that are important, not yours.

The Right Way: Identity and Security Based on Our Union with Christ

People who have a solid grasp on their identity in Christ walk through life with a sense of security and confidence that is rare and attractive to those who don't share in the same hope. This confidence comes from understanding and living their daily lives in light of the fact that God completely loves them and accepts them just as they are. They understand that God gives them both the desire and the power to grow spiritually. They understand that when God sees them, he sees the righteousness of Christ, and they thank him daily for that security. They rely on and daily depend on the Holy Spirit giving them both the motivation and the power to grow spiritually in all ways. Therefore, they experience gradual, but deep and lasting change rather than the false "instant sanctification" of sheer will power.

They feel no unhealthy sense of needing to "perform" in order to meet other people's approval. They don't wear masks and are completely comfortable sharing their opinion, even in groups where their particular beliefs might not be popular. They enjoy certain sports and hobbies but feel no sense of pressure to perform in order for others to admire them. In fact, they don't have any pressing need to be admired. They are completely content and secure in the love of their Father in heaven.

They sacrificially serve and love others in fresh and practical ways on a daily basis. There are times when they are mistreated, even abused by other people. Because of their security in Christ, they aren't devastated by someone being mean to them. They might be disappointed and even a bit hurt, but their world isn't shattered. They courageously share with the other person how their behavior is damaging and hurtful and firmly, but lovingly, suggest ways to improve. They do their part in helping guide people toward healthier interrelations, but they don't take personal responsibility for those who choose not to change. They seem to spend a lot of time thinking about creative ways to encourage other people without expecting anything in return. Theirs is a life that others notice, a security that all of us long for.

If this identity in Christ is such a powerful and authentic way to grow in your relationship with Christ, you might be thinking, *Where do I sign up? How do I get started?* Let's explore some practical ways to help our teens fully grasp who they are in Christ.

1. Do a study with them about the identity and security verses in Scripture.

   The Bible is filled with verses that talk about our identity in Christ. What better way to help your teenager get a clearer understanding of their identity in Christ than to sit down with them once a week for thirty minutes and study these passages together? Below, I will give you a few passages and some ideas for studying them to get you started. Be sure to open each session praying together that God would give you both a deep understanding and ownership of the truths found in each of these passages. Don't design this study without an end in sight; rather, commit to studying four passages for four weeks in a row. Your teenager won't feel like they are committing to it for every week the rest of their life. Remember, slow and steady.

   Keep in mind that this might take some homework and research. We should put as much effort (hopefully more) into these studies as we would planning for a vacation, cutting coupons, or finding the best deal on car tires. You might have to borrow some commentaries from your church library or check out some great websites that will aid in your study (www.crosswalk.com; www.e-sword.net are great places to start. They include commentaries, study aids, and different versions of the Bible).

   It might also help to make an appointment with your pastor and walk through some of these questions with him for insight. Do whatever it takes to make this study clear and biblically accurate for you and your teenager. Also, be sure to do some of the actual homework with your teenager; it's good for them to see you exploring the implications of these truths and for them to join you in the exploration process. Perhaps this means that you turn off the television for a month and use that time studying with your teenager—do whatever it takes. This stuff is eternal and has eternal implications for both you and your teenager; get a hold of that truth before you go any farther. Remember, whatever it takes. Here are some passages and ideas to get you started.

Therefore, if anyone is in Christ, he is a new creation. The old has passed away; behold, the new has come.

2 Corinthians 5:17

Questions to discuss:

- How does one come to the place of being "in Christ"?

- In what ways do we become a new creation?

- What about our "old self" has passed away?

I have been crucified with Christ. It is no longer I who live, but Christ who lives in me. And the life I now live in the flesh I live by faith in the Son of God, who loved me and gave himself for me.

Galatians 2:20

Questions to discuss:

• In what ways have you been crucified with Christ?

• How can you allow the Holy Spirit to help you become more like Christ by applying faith?

• Discuss how valuable you must be to God for him to give his Son for you.

As far as the east is from the west, so far does he remove our transgressions from us.

Psalm 103:12

Questions to discuss:

• According to this passage, once God has forgiven us for a particular sin, does he ever bring it up again?

• If God doesn't see our sin when he sees us, what does he see (Ephesians 4:24)?

• If God doesn't dig up our past sins, why is it harmful and bad for us to wallow in our past sins and beat ourselves up for them?

So that Christ may dwell in your hearts through faith—that you, being rooted and grounded in love, may have strength to comprehend with all the saints what is the breadth and length and height and depth, and to know the love of Christ that surpasses knowledge, that you may be filled with all the fullness of God.

Ephesians 3:17–19

Questions to discuss:

• If you know that someone loves you uncon-
ditionally, no matter what, how does that change how you feel around them (give specific examples)?

• How does the love of Christ surpass knowledge in the way that he feels about you?

• How does understanding how much God loves you, and the fact that it's unconditional, affect the way that you live and feel about God?

These passages and questions are just a few ideas to get you started. Consider finding Scripture-based books that talk about our identity and security in Christ and read them chap-
ter by chapter with your teenager. You might even have a weekly family book club. It's also helpful to encourage your teenager to teach these concepts to other teenagers in order for her to further develop her understanding and ownership of these deep and rich truths.

2. Memorize with them identity and security verses.

I've seen and experienced a strong and consistent Scripture memory program literally change people's personalities, break addictions, replace rage with joy...the miracles and stories are endless. Scripture memorization helps us lift Scripture off the page and place it into our hearts. There is something unique and powerful that happens in this process. God fuses his Word to our hearts, soul, and spirit in such a way that it literally changes our spiritual DNA. It gives the Holy Spirit living inside of us ammunition to use as we are faced with tempting situations and thoughts. Simply put, it replaces our inaccurate thoughts and beliefs with the truth of God's Word, and that is nothing short of transformational. Memorizing verses that give us an accurate picture of our identity and security in Christ is an absolute must. Spend time with your teenager finding these passages and then memorize them together.

3. Pray with and for them about their identity in Christ.

We must not neglect bringing the power of God into this process. Much of your time discipling your teenager should be spent on your knees, alone in your prayer closet (for me it's the laundry room). It's also important to pray with your spouse about your teenager. It needs to be a consistent time of prayer every day. Nothing unleashes the power of God more. Here are some ideas to supplement your prayer time:

• Pray for God to make his truths come alive in

your teenager's life in ways that he or she will clearly understand.

•Pray for God to give your teenager a hunger for his Word and for prayer. Often, people don't realize that God not only gives us resources for spiritual growth (Holy Spirit, Scripture, prayer, other believers, etc.), he also gives us the desire to grow spiritually. We need simply to ask.

•Pray that your teenager would be grounded in God's love, so that he or she can actually comprehend it in a way that will affect his or her life. Paul prayed this same prayer for the people in Ephesus (Ephesians 3:14–19).

•Pray that God would enable you to accurately model and share with your teenager what the unconditional love and acceptance of God looks like.

4. Model God's love and acceptance of them.

My wife and I are the proud parents of a beautiful baby daughter. I'm not afraid to admit that I have a baby crush. She is the most adorable little thing that I've ever seen. A lot of folks ask me if she's going to be a basketball player one day. She's already tall and slim like her daddy (I'm six foot seven inches and played basketball in college). I have a scripted answer, "She will play basketball if she wants to." Or she could be in the orchestra if she wants...or ballet....or [on the] speech team...or [in the] chess club. My acceptance and love for her isn't based on what she does or how she performs. It's not even based on her character.

> My acceptance and love for her is based on the
> fact that she is my daughter, period.

Many parents flirt dangerously close to having their teenagers believe that they are accepted or rejected, even in the most subtle ways, by how well they perform at the Friday night football game, or by whether or not their name is on some list that indicates how good their grades are. It's a good thing to teach our teenagers to work hard in all they do, it's biblical, but it's *not* biblical for them to believe that how they perform in any area of their life has the potential to change how we feel about them or see them or, worse yet, how God sees them.

My goal is to find the positive in anything that my daughter does. I will make darn sure that she feels no sense of needing to perform to meet my approval or acceptance. If she plays basketball, and they get beat one hundred to twenty-five, I will find a way to show her in a way that she understands that it doesn't change a thing about how I view her or think about her. Don't get me wrong, sometimes there will be opportunities to teach them about character issues, like not giving up or playing hard until the game is over no matter what the score, but we must be very clear and creative in making sure our teens understand that our love and acceptance of them exists without conditions.

Perhaps it's taking them out for ice cream after the game and telling them how proud you are of them for the way they respectfully treated the referees. Perhaps it's simply asking them if they tried their hardest when they didn't make the honor roll, and if they say yes, saying something like, "I never doubted for a moment that you did. I'm proud of you." Their success in this area is mostly dependent on you modeling it for them. Teenagers view God through the filter of their parents. If you model rejection for them, they will see God through that filter and probably have resentment for him like they do for you.

I hope that gets you started on helping your teenager understand his identity in Christ. This is the only place to start when discipling your teenager. If they don't understand this concept, they will have trouble with everything else. It's foundational and essential. Plead with God to help you teach and model it effectively.

What's the Holy Spirit's Role in Spiritual Growth?

I accepted Jesus Christ as my savior when I was in first grade, but I didn't allow Jesus to be Lord of my life until I was in college. Thus began a great struggle for me, something that kept me up for many nights worrying about my salvation; I couldn't stop cussing. I tried everything. I made New Year's resolutions to stop cussing, I told my accountability partner to punch me every time he heard me cuss, I put a rubber band around my wrist and snapped myself whenever I'd drop a verbal bomb, but nothing worked. I was discouraged and began to feel like I was a spiritual failure.

One day it happened in a dramatic fashion. I was walking into my dorm with a new basketball recruit, and I let loose some verbal pollution. He just looked at me, puzzled, and said, "You should really stop cussing so much." I felt embarrassed and ashamed. I remember agreeing with him out loud and then sitting in my dorm room asking God to help me stop cussing. As I look back, that was the first time that I actually asked God for his help in that area. Just like that, it was over. Cussing hasn't been a major stumbling block in my life since that prayer. I want to caution you here that sometimes we, as Christians, can be hypersensitive about language, even to the point of discounting someone's relationship with Christ if their language isn't as refined as we'd like. That is dangerous. Always remember that Jesus was mostly concerned with the heart of a person.

Sometimes language gives us insight into someone's heart, but we should never fall into the trap of "majoring on the minors." Language, in many cases, is a "minor."

That is a dramatic and easy example, and most struggles with sin aren't that simple, but the principle is loud and clear: we can't become godly and experience real and lasting spiritual growth under our own strength. The resources required for such deep and lasting growth are beyond our human capacity, and that is where understanding the role of the Holy Spirit becomes vitally important.

The Holy Spirit is God himself, living in and through us. He literally gives us the guidance, strength, and capacity to take on more and more of the characteristics and thought patterns that Jesus Christ had while he walked the earth. The Holy Spirit is our constant companion and helper when it comes to authentic spiritual growth.

Attempting to grow spiritually under our own volition becomes increasingly frustrating and disempowering. Growing by "walking according to the Spirit" yields the fruit of lasting change and peace. How do we open ourselves up to the guidance and power that God has given us in the person of the Holy Spirit? That's what we'll be looking at in this chapter.

Thinking About the Right Things

If you follow Jesus through the gospels, you will observe that he majors on internal things rather than external, and that is where spiritual growth begins. If we want to change our lives, we must first change our habits. If we want to change our habits, we must first change our actions. If we want to change our actions, we must first change our thoughts.

Romans 12:2 states quite clearly where we are to begin when it comes to partnering with the Holy Spirit in our spiritual growth,

> Do not be conformed to this world, but be
> transformed by the renewal of your mind, that
> by testing you may discern what is the will of
> God, what is good and acceptable and perfect.

Do not be conformed to this world.

We are living in what must be one of the most difficult times in history for teenagers. They are presented every day with a smorgasbord of conflicting ideas and messages. They are being taught about evolution in school. They watch soft pornography on their local cable network. They listen to violent and sensual lyrics on their MP3 players. They are preached to by politicians about the rights of every person to marry whomever they wish, even if the other person is of the same gender. They walk through the halls of their schools filled with teenagers who dress as though Eve never ate the apple ("I heard the sound of you in the garden, and I was afraid, because I was naked, and I hid myself."–Eve's hubby). We have no shame, no boundaries, no sense of obligation to live a holy and pure life.

As parents, we have two responsibilities in this area:

1. Protect our teenagers from things that they aren't mature enough to discern or handle by themselves yet.

2. Equip our teens to see the world around them through a biblical filtering system.

Protect our teenagers from things that they aren't mature enough to discern or handle by themselves yet.

This requires common sense and prayer. Every teenager is different, so every parent must discern the proper boundaries for their teens. This requires intentional and honest conversation, as well as lots of prayer. Of course, the younger the child, the stricter and shorter the leash of freedom.

For example, many teens are capable and mature enough to have their own online web page or journal, but many aren't. As their parents, you need to discern the level of your teenager's maturity and think carefully about some of the dangers of having such an online account. This will require lots of homework and discussion with your spouse and teenager. You don't want to shelter them from the world—that's just as bad—you just want to discern their ability to choose wisdom in certain situations and set them up for success.

The point is to take very seriously your responsibility to stand on the wall between your teenager and the things he isn't strong enough to handle on his own yet. Other common sense things might apply here, such as not renting a movie with sexually suggestive material in it when you have a male teenager living anywhere within seventeen miles of your home. Do not allow your daughter to have an emotionally intimate relationship with another male. There is no right or wrong answer to these hard questions; much time on your knees in prayer will be required, and you must come to an agreement with your spouse. It's important that you both are on board in order to maximize the effectiveness of the boundaries set.

Equip our teens to see the world around them through a biblical filtering system.

There is another extreme that is just as dangerous as allowing anything and everything to enter into your teenager's head, and that is to over-shelter your teenager. It creates a sense of unhealthy dependence on you as their parent. Don't do that. Remember, your main goal as a parent is to build them into strong and mature young adults. If you never give them room to make wise decisions using their own discernment, they won't be equipped to do so when you're not around. Allow room for failure—not major failure, like going away for the weekend without locking your wine cellar. We're talking small things at first, such as having your daughter think of a fair time for her curfew. You can guide her in this discussion, but you need to help her to start thinking as a responsible young person. If you don't allow them some room to make decisions while they're still living at home under your gracious supervision, they'll go off the deep end, making unwise decisions once they go to college or the "real world." Don't be afraid of every TV show, book, movie, or rock group; give your teenager some space to discern for themselves what is wise and unwise.

Guide your teenager gently while standing in the background on most things. Remember, there is no formula for helping your teenagers think biblically, because it's a heart issue. Ultimately, you want your teenager to own their convictions; you don't want them to leech off of your convictions—that's not spiritually healthy for them. You must be gentle and gracious, talking them through it. The more your teenager strays from a godly path, the less you preach, and the closer you walk beside them. The principle is summed up in the book *Emotionally Intelligent Parenting*, "Adolescents will often bait parents with this kind of purposeful rejection of parental values in their attempt to establish their own identities."[5] The key is to love them, accept them, and consider other areas where you can give them freedom to establish their own identities apart from yours—areas where you might differ in taste and personality, rather than morals and beliefs. For instance, let him get the crazy Mohawk haircut. Let her pierce her bellybutton. In light of eternity, who really cares? It gives your teenager a much safer release for establishing a separate identity from her parents, rather than rejecting her parents' faith altogether for the sake of identity.

Keep in mind, when your teenager begins to stray from God, it's easier to steer him with your arm beside him, letting him know you care, than it is to shout commandments from the hilltops. So when your teenagers begin to slip (and they will), get more involved in their lives. Encourage them more. Love them more. Walk closer, and in so doing, you will earn the right to help influence, guide and direct.

Grace and Avoiding Exasperation

According to Ephesians 6:4, it is a sin for parents to exasperate their children. Here's how dictionary.com defines exasperate: "To make very angry or impatient; annoy greatly."[6] Think about it, God has commanded us not to annoy our teenagers. That's a pretty heavy statement, but I really believe that God says what he means and means what he says. If we are continually exasperating our teenagers, nagging them about every little thing, we will eventually lose significant relational capital. If we lose relational capital with our teenagers, they begin to hide things from us and lose all concern for our thoughts and opinions on their lives. The more we exasperate our teenagers, the greater the gulf between them and us, emotionally, mentally, even physically.

Let's discover some practical ways to avoid exasperating your teenager by utilizing a grace-centered approach.

Use Conversations for Connection

I think a great place to start is to have daily doses, small at first, of meaningful conversation with your teenager. I think it would be a mistake to attempt to manufacture authentic conversation with your teenagers if they're not used to having authentic dialogue with you. In this case, the best place to start having conversations with them is whenever and wherever they want to talk. This is where you must be flexible and fluid. You just got home from the grocery store, and you are exhausted. The car needs to be unloaded because it's ninety degrees outside and the milk is going bad. Your teenage daughter enthusiastically greets you at the door and says, "Guess what!" She has something exciting to tell you, but the milk is going bad in the car. Do you tell her to hold on and unload the groceries first? No! Not if you're looking for ways to bridge the communication gulf between you and your daughter. You sit down. Enthusiastically engage in conversation with your daughter. Ask her a ton of questions. And then you thank her for sharing. (Then you go buy some more milk.) Think about it…that is a priceless moment, I would rather you go spend another hundred bucks or so on all the groceries that went bad in your trunk. For heaven's sake, engage with your teenagers on their terms if you expect to build enough relational capital to talk about the bigger stuff later.

These conversations might seem trivial and unimportant at first, but what might seem unimportant to you could be the very thing that your teenager needs in order to build trust for tackling bigger areas and longer conversations. Teens become exasperated with their parents when they don't feel listened to or understood. These harmful feelings are the building blocks for the walls they place between themselves and their parents when it comes to authentic conversations.

Jay McGraw said, "If you don't talk to your kids about the little stuff, they won't talk to you about the big stuff."[7] I think there's a lot of wisdom in that statement. It would be worth asking yourself how much interest you take in the "little stuff" that your teens are interested in—hobbies, sports, friends, etc.

Meaningful conversation, if made into a habit and then a lifestyle, will develop a mutual respect and appreciation.

This, in turn, will open up the door for you to have greater influence in the life of your teenager.

Dr. Henry Cloud, in his wonderful book called *Integrity*,[8] talks about the importance of building connections with people you hope to influence. He says that without truly connecting with someone, you will not have any lasting influence on the person's life. This is just as true in parenting as it is in the business world or church. True, some parents can bully their way to their teenager's compliance without any true connection, but it's an empty commitment on their teenager's part. In other words, they'll comply, they'll go through the motions while you're watching, but as the resentment grows, so does the level of rebellion when they go off to college, to work, or to their friend's house. Dr. Cloud says that connection happens when you enter into another person's reality, validate it and treat it with respect.

I've seen parents fail in this arena many times. A teenager will be expressing his concerns, frustrations, or feelings, and the parent quickly and harshly interrupts, demanding an apology for "disrespectful language." There was nothing disrespectful about the language or the tone of the teenager, he was simply sharing his real feelings. On top of that, when he apologizes, the parent demands that he do it again, this time with a smile. Give me a break, I'm an advocate for parents and will always side with the parent over the teenager, but that almost drives me up the wall. How can you expect your teenager to be real with you when you condition him to act when he's trying to be authentic. Don't do that parents; please, don't do that.

We as parents also make the mistake of unintentionally invalidating what our teenagers say during the course of a conversation. I remember making a home visit to one of our fringe teenagers who hadn't been to any of our youth ministry events in a while. I sat down with his family for dinner, and my heart absolutely ached as I heard the father invalidate his son's comments one after another. You could see his son deflating before our very eyes. He wanted to go to college; his dad thought it was a bad idea and wanted him to pursue work. He wanted to play football; his dad said that it wasn't a worthy goal. He talked about books he was reading; his dad asked how he had time for reading when he wasn't even doing his homework. I felt like laying hands on his father...in Christian love. He was teaching his son that dreaming, setting goals, and sharing his hopes and desires wasn't acceptable behavior.

We must listen to our teenagers. We must look them in the eye when they're talking with us. We must affirm their authentic sharing and ask questions that prove we're really listening. Our goal is this: while they are talking with us, they truly believe that nothing in the world is more important to us than the conversation we are having with them at that moment. Nothing.

Teaching through Conversation

You might not agree with or approve of everything your teenager says; that's not the point. In fact, they won't even consider your input in a conversation unless they first feel truly understood by you. It's true that it is your responsibility to guide them in making wise decisions, but guiding doesn't mean coming into a conversation with your guns loaded and shoving a twenty-minute sermon down their throat without ever giving them room to share feelings and thoughts. Guiding is all about asking the right questions; it means that you train them to think things through before jumping to a decision. Here's what that might look like in a typical conversation:

"Dad, I think I'm going to get a tattoo on my neck."

"Hmm, that's interesting. Tell me something, buddy, how much thought have you put into this?"

"Well, I've been thinking about design, and I think I

finally decided on getting the Japanese Kanji character for the word 'courage.'"

"I think 'courage' is definitely a valuable and godly characteristic; let's come back to that in a second. When I asked how much thought you'd put into this, I wasn't referring to what tattoo you were interested in getting, I was actually asking how much thought you had put into the implications of getting a tattoo on your neck."

"Oh, implications, shimplications..."

Chuckling. "No I'm serious, son. Let's spend some time walking through this thing together. One of my jobs as your Pops is to help you have a bigger perspective on things, so let's take a closer look at this whole tattoo thing. First of all, *why* is it that you're so interested in getting a tattoo on your neck?"

"To be honest, I haven't thought a whole lot about that; I just think it would add to my image, something unique. I'm my own man, and I think it would be cool to have a tattoo there."

"Okay, son, I realize that I'm way out of date here, so I guess I'm just going to need your help with this whole 'cool' thing. What does it mean to be cool these days?"

"I don't know, Dad, come on. I guess it's just an image thing, you know? It's just about being your own man, doing what you want to do and not caring what anyone else thinks. That's cool."

"So I guess the question is this, do you *really* not care what people think if you are getting a tattoo on your neck for the sake of other people seeing it and it adding to your image?"

"Okay, Columbo."

"Ha ha ha...seriously, stay with me on this one. Okay, here's another question, remember the other day you said you were interested in going into business school?"

"Yeah..."

"What type of image do you want to portray when

you walk into that interview room on Wall Street in five years?"

"I don't know, I guess I want them to think that I'm competent, that I'm on top of my game, that I'm a professional."

"I think those are all great things, buddy, and I think, as wrong as it might seem, it's still reality that people will judge you in those areas by your appearance. What might someone who doesn't know you think about your level of professionalism when they see you walk into the interview room with a suit on and a giant tattoo on your neck?"

"I guess they might not think that's too cool."

"Yeah, maybe not. Plus, what will that thing look like in fifty years all wrinkly...ha ha ha. Do you think it might be a good idea to put that one on the shelf for now?"

"Yeah, I think probably so."

"Great, so let's talk about this courage thing now..."

Now, perhaps the content of this example doesn't apply to you. I really don't know if God cares either way if your son gets a tattoo on his neck. The point is that as a parent, using your best judgment, your job is to guide your teenager in making wise decisions by asking astute questions. This process is best guided by a complete and utter dependence on the Holy Spirit and tons of prayer.

Now compare that gracious and gentle conversation with the more exasperating and common version:

"Dad, I think I'm going to get a tattoo on my neck."

"Oh, that would just be dumb. You would regret that later in life, I guarantee it."

"No, I wouldn't; besides, that would be my problem, not yours."

"Well, it's my problem right now, so as long as you're living under my roof, you are *not* getting a tattoo. Why on earth would you want to do something like that anyways?"

"I don't know, I just think that it..."

"The answer's no. End of discussion, period."

Talk about exasperating. The father never even listened to his son. He never encouraged his son to think through the implications on his own. He never asked for his opinion or thoughts. He didn't give his son any room to express his feelings. He never affirmed or validated him in any way. Instead, Dad gave him a list of rules and clear instructions: *the answer is no.*

What could have been an authentic conversation turned into an opportunity for Dad to make his own feelings and rules very clear...without having to go through the emotional waste of energy of ever having to really connect with his son. My sarcasm becomes me.

Unfortunately, many of us are anemic when it comes to having authentic conversations with our teenagers. Let me suggest two other ways we can maximize our conversations with our teenagers:

1. Be there, and be prepared to be nowhere else.[9] Don't look at your watch. Don't interrupt to yell for someone in the next room over. Don't interrupt them, period. Don't answer your cell phone. Don't think about what you're going to make for dinner. Don't glaze over.

   Conversations are serious business. If you aren't prepared to engage one hundred percent in the conversation, don't even bother. Your job as a parent is to sit in front of your teenager, eyeball to eyeball, and convince her that you believe that, at that moment, nothing in the world is more important than what she has to say. Her feelings and words are all that you care about. For all you know, the rest of the world is falling apart all around you. Put the remote control down, put the newspaper down...for God's sake (I'm speaking literally there) engage with your teenager.

2. Don't think of what you're going to say next while they're talking.

Sometimes our conversations need to be direct and guided. Sometimes we need to rebuke, correct, or train. Sometimes we need to get to the point, but most times not.

Susan Scott, in her book Fierce Conversations, tells us that each of our realities change on a daily basis, and our job is to make sure that we sit down long enough with each other to keep up with each other's realities. Now hear me out here, I'm not talking about macro-reality as it pertains to our relationship to and with Jesus Christ, who is our ultimate reality. I'm talking about experiential reality.

Experiential reality simply put is the way that we are affected by things that happen to us. Many couples don't take the time to check in with each other's experiential realities, and it destroys their marriage. For instance, Mr. Smith says something sarcastically to his wife, because that's how his parents related to him growing up. He has no clue that, when he leaves for work, Mrs. Smith cries for an hour, deeply wounded by his off-handed remarks. Mr. Smith comes home, watches TV, kisses his wife goodnight, and goes to bed. The trend continues until one day he comes home to a note and an empty house. All because they never took the time to connect with each other. She never sat down and shared her feelings about how deeply hurtful his words were to her. We are obligated to make sure that we tell each other where we are in the relationship and in life. We must make the time to keep up to speed with what's going on inside each others' heads. Mr. Smith never took the time.

This is an oversimplified example, I know, but I think you get the picture. We must make it a priority to have daily "check ins" with our teenagers. We must give them space and opportunity to air what they're feeling and experiencing. We must reserve judgment or punishment for what they tell us. We must ask them where and how they are in life and mean it.

I suggest having a time each day where you can truly connect with your teenagers, be it at the dinner table, sitting on their bed talking and praying with them before they doze off, turning off the TV to play cards, or doing an activity together that gives room for conversation...whatever it takes.

You may want to ease into this habit; it could be intimidating and overwhelming at first for your teenager, but you must lovingly persist and admit that it feels awkward, but you really value them and want to make some changes in order to keep up with each other's lives. This means that you should share as well. Here are some ideas to get the conversations rolling—use one of them, all of them, none of them—they're just ideas to get you thinking. Perhaps you could rotate one per evening, and then pray with your teenager about what they share. One more tip. When I was in journalism class in high school, my teacher taught us to never be satisfied with the first answer, always work for the second. To experience real success in this exercise, follow up with another question about the answer they share. It could lead to some great conversation and insight. Here are some ideas to get you started:

- What in your life is most frustrating for you right now?

- If you could change anything about your life, what would it be?

- Where do you feel that I'm being unfair as a parent?

- If you could wake up tomorrow morning, ten years older, where would you be? Who would you be?

- What dream do you have that you've never shared with me?

- In eighty years, when your best friend (sister, boss, teacher, youth pastor, etc.) is speaking at your funeral, what would you want him to say about you?

Compel Them to Christ, Don't Push

When I was a teenager, I never went to youth group because I thought it was boring. Why did I think it was boring? Because most of the kids I knew who went to youth group were bored with their Christianity, so Christianity was in no way attractive to me. I wanted nothing to do with it. My parents could have forced me to go to youth group, as many parents do, but I think that's counterproductive. I can look at the faces of teens in my youth group and see who's there because they are compelled to be there, and who's there because their parents dragged them through the door kicking and screaming.

Frankly, I'd rather not have a kid there who doesn't want to be there. It's not helping any of the other kids because they're disruptive, and it's definitely not helping him; in fact, it's doing more harm than good for him. If a teenager feels forced to sit through Sunday school or whatever, they will naturally rebel and push against it. It's best to give them space and wear your knees out praying for them to see Christ as he really is and fall in love with him. You might even ask the youth director if there's an adult who works with the student ministry or a group of students that are already plugged in who might be interested in developing a relationship outside of the ministry with your son. Once that relationship is developed, with no strings attached, it will be a smoother and more natural transition to plug into the student ministry. Don't force it; the relationships must come first.

If you want to see your teenager experiencing a vibrant, zealous, fulfilling life in Christ, you had better make sure that that is exactly what you are seeing in the mirror. If you're bored with your own walk with Christ, how on earth do you expect your teenager to be attracted to it? This is where you have to man up (or woman up), and be realistic about your personal walk. What does your daily time with God look like? Are you just trudging through the Bible, or is it becoming more and more alive with your disciplined and consistent study and reading time? Are you hiding his Word in your heart through Scripture memorization? Is your prayer life dull and repetitious or fresh, powerful, and contagious? Do you have a plan to take as many people to heaven with you as possible? Do you have non-Christian friends who you are regularly exposing to Christ's love and truth? Does Jesus affect every area of your life? Are you experiencing the fruits of the Spirit? Do you accept and embrace the challenge of the slow, but deep, process of spiritual growth into maturity? Do you sit in a pew on Sunday morning, or are you a part of a moving, breathing, dynamic, living body of Christ? Is your faith attractive to your teenager?

Part of your job as a parent is to model an adventurous faith for your teenager and invite them to come along with you. We have no excuse for being bored Christians. Jesus was the furthest thing from boring. Teaching should involve both study and action, scholarly yet practical. A lot of teenagers know the Bible fairly well (relatively speaking); they can even quote Scripture. Most teenagers are exposed to decent Bible teaching, but they just never do anything with it. All the information and Scripture comes in, but they keep it inside, never doing anything with it. It's called "knowledge constipation." We need to equip our teens to learn a principle from Scripture and then, with the help of the Holy Spirit, apply it to their lives in a real way. Perhaps some ideas might help.

1. I got this idea from Mike Nygren, founder of the School of Urban Studies. He's a friend and ministry coach. Take your teenager to a soup kitchen, be sure to wear clothes that might resemble those of the people you'll be dining with. That's right, you're not going to the soup kitchen to serve, you're going there to eat. It's easy for teenagers to stand behind a table and serve soup from a kettle. In fact, I can convince any teenager to spend at least one afternoon doing that. Soup servers are a dime a dozen. The real challenge comes when you decide to help meet another need in the lives of the families and individuals who attend soup kitchens—their feeling of having dignity.

   One conversation could go a long way for both your teenager and the person they sit down with to eat. Teach your teenager to ask questions that won't be insulting or presumptuous. Many of these folks haven't had a conversation with their son or daughter or grandkids in years. Many folks started out just like you and I but hit some bad bumps in the road and are now alone. There are also cases of addiction and mental disorders, so don't be naïve, but do be gracious. Having these conversations will not only give the other person a sense of dignity and respect, it will also help your teenager to have a sense of other people's needs and hurts. Anything we can do to help our teenagers move their focus from themselves to others is a huge step.

Put on some unassuming clothes, convince your daughter to not wear makeup, jewelry, or do her hair for this one time, and go find yourself a soup kitchen. Stand in line with everyone else. Accept the soup with everyone else. Sit down with everyone else, and let God go to work. If you really want to do this right, study the background, history, dynamics, and social implications of homeless people and the welfare system. Study how Jesus met people's needs with your teenagers, and how he says we should steward what we've been given in order to help others. Look at passages like James 1:27 and ask your teenager why God included visiting orphans and widows in their affliction as something that God considers to be "pure and undefiled religion before God." Why is it important to do things for people who can't give anything in return?

2. Study Scripture and read books about fasting. Then go on a four-day fast with your teenager. Make a list of things that you will pray about both individually and together. Be sure to discuss together what the real purpose of fasting is.

3. Study 1 Corinthians 9:24–27 with your teenager. Talk about what it means to discipline yourself. Talk about how self-control is important in your spiritual life, how a godly person lives a controlled and disciplined life (2 Timothy 1:7 also might be helpful). Here's the kicker, while studying this passage and these thoughts, choose a marathon date in the not so distant future, register you and your teenager so there's no turning back, and begin training with your teenager. Keep passages about discipline and buffeting your body and self control and all that fun stuff in front of you at all times. Memorize them, breath them, live them. At the end, you should celebrate together by running in a marathon with each other. She'll never forget it, and the Scripture will come alive through the pain and triumph.

The point is to be creative. Creativity and adventure are two of my main life values simply because I think that Christians are getting too boring, and it's a major turnoff for nonbelievers. The true "draw" of Christianity is the life-saving and giving relationship with Jesus Christ, but there's nothing wrong with enjoying your walk. Like Howard Hendricks says to grumpy and dull Christians, who wear their "Christian sufferings" on their faces like badges of honor, "I know you're a Christian, but you don't have to look like one."

Nurturing a Love for God's Word

Cultivating a love for God's Word in the heart of a teenager is no easy task. In fact, it's impossible without God's divine intervention. We start with prayer. Loud, meaningful, heartfelt prayer. We must ask God to give our teenagers a burning desire for his Word.

Then we look in the mirror again, and we ask ourselves some more hard questions. How is your own personal Scripture intake program? Are you just reading and neglecting studying? Are you just studying and neglecting getting an overview of God's Word by reading? Are you consistent? Do you have a regular time? Is it a five-minute devotional or daily thought that someone else wrote, or are you eating firsthand from God's Word? Do you study and read when you don't feel like studying and reading? What's your Scripture memory program? How seriously do you take God's Word? Really?

It is vital that we are growing in our understanding and application of God's Word in our own lives if we have those expectations for our teenagers.

I teach out of the Bible every weekend to teenagers. I know when I'm connecting, and I know when I'm flopping. Teaching Scripture to teenagers is one of the hardest things I've ever had to do on a consistent basis. There is no faking. There's no fooling them if you aren't one hundred percent sold on what you're trying to sell them. If it's not real and alive in your own life, you're a sham, and teenagers can smell shams from a mile away.

Many of us have grown up with *the hand* illustration made popular by the Navigators. It simply illustrates that in order to have a complete grip on what the Bible has for us, it's important to an intake strategy that includes five different approaches, all of them are important.

As you're reading this section, please remember that helping your teenager develop spiritual disciplines won't (and shouldn't) happen if you force them into a rigid structure or method. Every teenager is different, and you must take the time to pray about them and study them. Pray that God would give you creative ideas to turn your teenager on to spiritual growth. Study them carefully. This isn't about haphazardly throwing information and habits at them; it's intentionally helping them discover what works best for them.

Somehow, someway, somewhere, there is a method of Bible intake and prayer that will awaken them to the things of God. You're job as a parent is to care enough about this stuff to help them un-earth the treasure (which, in this case, is the method that works for them). Not everyone should do their Bible reading at oh-dark-thirty in the morning. Some teenagers are night owls, and it would be best for them to read the Bible late in the evening. Not everyone can sit at a table in the kitchen to pray. Some teenagers need to be walking through the woods, enjoying God's creation as they pray. Remember, we're trying to prime the pump. Yes, it's important that your teenager learns to pray in all ways, at all times, and in all places. We're simply helping cultivate the habit and desire. This is why it's important to study your teenager.

If I had a teenager who jogged every morning at 5:30 a.m. (seriously, I know a few who do), I would encourage her to listen to a few chapters of the Bible on her iPod, then spend some time thinking about what she listened to and pray it as she's showering. If I had a teenager who enjoyed the water, I would buy a sailboat and call it "Quiet Time," and that is where I'd teach him how to study Scripture and fish for men. If I had a teenager who enjoyed creative writing, I would have him rewrite in his own words some passages in Scripture. Of course, we would first have to discover the heart of the passage, what it originally meant, in order for him to craft his work. If I had a son who enjoyed working with his hands and wood, carpentry, I would build a prayer kneeler with him. He could craft it however he chooses and then use it for a daily time in prayer and thinking about God's Word. Or perhaps I would build a tree house with my daughters, and there they could memorize God's Word and hide it in their heart. If they were musicians, I would study God's grace with them and ask them to write a song about the unfailing and unfading grace of God. The point is to be creative. Don't just give them rigid habits to add to their daily schedule; help it to be somewhat organic and natural.

Let's explore the H.A.N.D. illustration together.

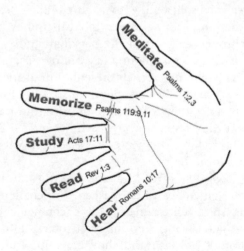

Hear

> So faith comes from hearing, and hearing
> through the word of Christ.
>
> Romans 10:17

I don't speak Greek, Aramaic, or Hebrew. I know how to use a concordance, that's about it. I enjoy learning about historical and cultural context of biblical writings, but I don't have a lot of time to study them on my own. Quite frankly, I wouldn't even know where to start. This is where those folks who stand in front of crowds on Sunday mornings or evenings come in handy. They've read the books. They've gone through seminary training. They've had to learn Greek and Hebrew and historical context. The major focus of their job is to study thoroughly and teach clearly the truths of the Bible. They are literally paid to spend hours and hours of study and preparation time to ensure that what they are teaching is accurate. There is nothing more powerful than hearing God's Word preached in a crystal clear and compelling manner.

Often times, listening to a gifted Bible teacher will prime the pump for your own biblical studies. When I'm going through a desert in my personal studies, I'll commit to listening for an hour a day online to someone who really challenges me in their presentation of the Word. I'll do this systematically for a month or so, listening to either a topical series they're teaching or an entire book of the Bible that they systematically teach. It works every time! I approach my Bible study after those seasons with renewed vigor and thoroughness.

We need to be careful here; notice that I'm not saying I'm "entertained" by these speakers, I'm challenged. Bible teaching isn't to entertain us, it's to encourage us on toward love and good works. Too many of today's Bible teachers are majoring on flash and showmanship. Too few Bible teachers are consistently taking their listeners to a deeper and more complete understanding of God's Word.

Another idea to consider is purchasing for your teenager the Bible on CD. Encourage them to listen as they're driving or have a designated family listening time. Perhaps this could become a family ritual. Go through the New Testament listening to one chapter each night before settling in for bed, then briefly discuss any observations or comments. End with a quick prayer. It doesn't need to be a lot. Too much might turn them off. You teach someone to eat by giving them tiny bites, a little at a time. Imagine trying to teach your infant how to eat adult food by giving her a steak to munch on. It doesn't work very well.

Read

> Blessed is the one who reads aloud the words
> of this prophecy.
>
> Revelation 1:3a

I enjoy the story of Billy Graham talking about his Bible reading plan with Johnny Carson. He said that he always reads a chapter in the Old Testament and a chapter in the New Testament, including at least one chapter in the Gospels. The reason, he said, was to make sure that he was never too far from the life of Jesus. I think there is great wisdom in that method.

There are many ways to approach a Bible reading plan; the key is that you *have* a plan to begin with and that it's consistent. I think it's important to have some type of reading plan that takes you through the entire Bible. There are great Bibles that are specifically designed to help you read the Bible in a year or two. Keep in mind that your level of spiritual maturity isn't determined by how long it takes you to read through the Bible, as long as you have a systematic method to get through the Bible. Perhaps you're up for reading three or four chapters a day, perhaps you struggle just reading one. Give your teenager permission to go at their pace.

One of the more powerful methods I've used in my own personal devotions is simply reading the Bible aloud until "I'm struck." That simply means to read until something strikes you as particularly interesting. At that point, I reread the verse or two that struck me, close my Bible, pray about the verse, and then spend time throughout the day thinking about the verses. Right now I'm reading through the Bible using D.A. Carson's *For the Love of God*.[10] I highly recommend it to those looking for a plan. Carson gives great insight into the daily passage but doesn't give a "devotional" thought; it's simply insight into the passage as it pertains to the overall scope of the Bible.

The point is to encourage your teenagers to do whatever works. Whatever method they choose, help them develop a systematic method of reading through the Bible in its entirety.

Study

> Now these Jews were more noble than those in Thessalonica; they received the word with all eagerness, examining the Scriptures daily to see if these things were so.
>
> Acts 17:11

One of the most popular classes at Dallas Theological Seminary is taught by Dr. Howard Hendricks, affectionately known as "Prof." Dr. Hendricks has been teaching at the seminary for over fifty years. The class is all about personal Bible study methods, and it charges the students to the core. I heard once that the first day of class, Dr. Hendricks asks the students to make twenty-five observations about Acts 1:8. The second day of class, he asks them to make twenty-five new observations about the same verse. The study of Scriptures is all about noting the obvious and then asking more penetrating, less obvious questions. It's not only studying the content of the passage, but also the structure of the book. It's about being a reporter on steroids...dig, dig, dig until you see the passage with fresh eyes.

The good news for the rest of us is that the material covered in Dr. Hendricks' popular class is available in a book written by Dr. Hendricks and his son called *Living by the Book*.

Buy it.

Read it.

Study it.

Your approach to Bible study will be changed forever!

Memorize

> I have stored up your word in my heart, that
> I might not sin against you.
>
> Psalm 119:11

When you memorize Scripture, you are literally taking God's words off the page and into your brain, pushing it down into the core of your inner man. This process changes you from deep inside.

It's also a way for us to combat our natural drift toward negativity, which leads to depression and anxiety. In Philippians 4:8, Paul is teaching us to be proactive in controlling what we allow ourselves to think about. Scripture is the most powerful and life-enhancing thing that we could possibly think about.

Despite all of this, most Christians don't give the mental energy needed to the discipline of memorizing Scripture.

I'll never forget a statement made by Peter J. Daniels, an ultra-successful Christian business man, "The secret of your success in life is determined by your ability to bear pain." Scripture memory is not something that usually yields instant results. Rather it's a discipline that, if cultivated, will pay off in the form of depth, peace, and real change in the long run. This presents a great opportunity for you to teach your teenagers the value of discipline for the sake of long-term results. Talk with them about some of the long-term benefits of planting God's Word deep in their minds. Talk about how it will help them have the courage to stand firm in their convictions. Talk about how it will literally change their desires from the things in the world that are destructive to things of God that lead to a more fulfilling and joyful life. Teach them to work through the desire to see instant results, cultivating a lifelong discipline of Scripture memory.

Some of you might not agree with this, but I don't think there's anything wrong with creating a reward system for Scripture memory. After all, God has given every Christian the challenge of working as hard as we can on this side of eternity to be about the business of making disciples—with the promise that the more lives we build into spiritually here on earth, the greater our rewards will be in heaven. Make one of those little charts where your teenager can put a star next to each verse they memorize, and brainstorm with your teenager about a reward that really gets their juices flowing. Sometimes external rewards are a way of providing motivation that isn't naturally inside of someone but keeps him going to the point where they *do* have intrinsic motivation.

As an example, last year I signed up to compete in a triathlon with my friend. I had very little internal motivation to train, but I had an abundance of external motivation in that I am very competitive. I wanted to finish in front of my friend. What I noticed is that at first, the only thing that got me to the gym was the external motivation of defeating my friend. Toward the end, I couldn't wait to get to the gym, and it had nothing to do with wanting to beat my friend. I was experiencing the real and powerful rewards of a disciplined exercise ritual. I was internally motivated to the nth degree. It has happened in every area my life.

Sit down with your teenager over some coffee and think of a reasonable memory program with an extravagant reward. Then pray like there's no tomorrow that God will develop in them an intrinsic desire for Scripture memorization.

Meditate

> But his delight is in the law of the Lord, and
> on his law he meditates day and night.
>
> Psalms 1:2

To meditate on Scripture simply means to think about it a lot. Think about it in the car. Think about it in the shower. Think about it while you're walking the dog. Think about it while you're making your bed. Think about it while you're eating. Think about it before you fall asleep at night. Think about it while you're brushing your teeth. Think about God's Word all the time. There is nothing more profitable to think about than God's Word. Nothing.

This is where you'll really need to be creative as a parent. You might want to sit down with your spouse and brainstorm different ways to make Scripture meditation a daily part of your teenager's life. Perhaps you have a family devotional time and give some questions at the end of the meeting for your teenagers to think about for a day or two. Perhaps you have a Bible book club, where everyone reads the same chapter in the Bible, and then over dinner everyone shares what captured their attention most in the chapter. Be creative.

Cultivating a Desire for Prayer

Someone once said the best thing about passion is that you can't hide it. The best way to teach someone how to pray passionately and authentically is to pray passionately and authentically with them. Prayer is an area that needs to be modeled. Unfortunately, too many of our churches are modeling anemic and repetitive prayers. Sadly, the language used during prayer time is formalized and seasoned with churchy words, words that many teens don't even understand. Some folks even lower their voices when they pray, as though God were looking for certain voice inflections. If it weren't so sad, it would be comical.

I have two goals for this chapter:

1. To help you design your own personal prayer strategy. Modeling is especially important when it comes to teaching your teenager how to pray.

2. To help you help your teenagers design their own prayer strategy.

Planned Prayer Times

Henry Cloud has wonderful insight on how to effectively utilize accountability. He says that it is futile to meet with a group of people and go through a checklist of questions. That always ends badly, with disillusion and heartbreak... not to mention many lost friendships. The true purpose of accountability is to provide someone external strength in an area where they don't have the internal strength to provide for themselves.[11]

For example, if someone asks me to hold him accountable to run every morning at 6 a.m., it would be pretty ineffective for me to just ask him every day if he ran. If he doesn't have the strength internally to roll out of bed and hit the road running, he's not going to do it on his own, period. The better thing would be for me to ring his doorbell at 5:50 a.m., roll him out of bed, and run *with* him. That would be an example of me providing external strength in an area where he doesn't have the internal strength to provide for himself. Eventually, by sheer habit and personal victories piling up, he will build the internal strength to do it on his own, and I can sleep in again. Actually, my brother-in-law did this very thing for one of his friends, and it was the only thing that worked in helping his friend develop the habit of exercising in the morning.

It's the same thing with prayer. Many of your teens don't have the internal strength to develop a consistent prayer time on their own. That's where you come in. Schedule a time with them every day to pray. Maybe it's right before bed or after breakfast. Whenever you choose, make it consistent, and do it with them even when they don't feel up to it, even when *you* don't feel up to it. Read books together on prayer. Ask God for the desire to pray. Just do it.

You might consider props such as praise music playing in the background, pillows to put under your knees if you're kneeling together in prayer (which I highly recommend), perhaps you'd even feel more comfortable with turning off all the lights. Whatever it takes, develop a consistent time with your teenager in prayer.

Spontaneous Prayer Times

Paul urges us in 1 Thessalonians 5:18 to spend time in prayer all throughout the day. A great way to cultivate the habit of praying spontaneously throughout the day is to utilize transition moments and "mindless" moments.

Transition moments are those margins of time between two activities. For instance, car rides are a great time for prayer. You're traveling from one destination or activity to another. What better time to thank God for his provision for your last activity and ask him for guidance in the next. Perhaps between classes as your teenager is walking through the halls, he might pray for courage to share his faith with the guy who sits next to him in biology.

A mindless moment is self-explanatory. Mindless moments come in two categories: during times of physical activity and during habitual moments. Physical activity provides a great time for prayer because most of the energy you are using is with your body, not your mind. If you're running five miles on the treadmill, you have a lot of time to think, better yet, a lot of time to pray. If you're lifting weights, chopping wood, or building a tree house...you may as well pray.

Habitual activities also provide a great space for prayer. Most teenagers spend at least fifteen minutes in the shower every day. Imagine adding fifteen minutes to your prayer time each day. Do you brush your teeth every day? You might as well be praying (you don't have to speak the words out loud to pray). The point is, there are plenty of times throughout the day to cultivate the habit of spontaneous prayer. This will lead to a better understanding of what it means to depend on God in all areas of life. There is no stronger person than that person who knows that he is nothing without the activity of God in his life.

Specific Tips for Helping Your Teenager with Her Prayer Life

1. Don't allow your teenager to pray with guilt. Many teenagers are way too hard on themselves when they speak to God. They talk about how horrible they are for not praying enough, and how long it's been since they last spoke with God. Encourage them to just skip through those rants and go right to thanking God for his grace and unconditional love.

2. Make prayer a normal part of your household life. It doesn't have to be a formal, "Dear Father..." You can just thank God aloud for random things throughout the day. Modeling gratitude toward God aloud and often is a wonderful gift and legacy to pass along to your teens. When Jesus was on earth, he wasn't easily surprised. Yet in Luke 17:11–19, Jesus seemed to be amazed at the ingratitude of nine of the ten lepers that he had healed. Only *one* came back to thank him. That's pretty ugly, yet how often do we forget to acknowledge and thank God for the things he's done for us?

3. Teach your teenager how to pray with maturity beyond just praying for your great aunt's friend's goldfish. If you're looking for things to pray, here are some places to start:

    a. Pray the promises of the Scripture.

    b. Pray the prayers modeled in the Bible (Jesus, Paul etc.).

c.Pray about a passage that stuck out in your devotional time with God.

d.Tell God about himself. Praise him for his characteristics (holy, perfect, merciful, creative, generous, loving, sovereign...).

Teaching Teenagers to Focus on Others, Not Themselves

Self-focused living is the greatest threat to the church in America today. I'm not talking about people outside of the church, I'm talking about people inside the church. We are giving our teenagers a horrible example when it comes to living for the sake of others. Let's address that problem before we go any farther.

Several years ago, I heard Walt Henrichsen give the best and simplest definition of love that I'd ever heard, "Love is simply doing what's best for the other."

Teenagers are inherently selfish. Well, we all are, but especially teenagers. As parents, one of our main goals should be to help build an others-focused mindset into our teens rather than self-focused.

When I take students on a mission trip, one of my goals is to break them of their self-focused way of thinking. Most teenagers ask the same questions:

- Can I bring my iPod?
- Can I bring my hair dryer and hair curler or hair straightener?
- Do we have to sleep on the floor, or can I bring an air mattress?
- Is the place where we're staying air-conditioned?
- Will we be able to take a shower every day?

- How much time will we have for free time?
- Are we going to be eating good food?

By the end of our trips, most of the teenagers have had a paradigm shift and realize how ridiculous and selfish these questions were. Most teenagers don't go on a mission trip to focus on serving other people; most teenagers go on a mission trip for a vacation time with their friends or to spend the rest of the year patting themselves on the back for how great they are for helping "those people." Nothing is more pitiful.

It takes some time and some breaking to help a teenager see that the world does not, should not, and never will revolve around their comfort. It is up to us to help them see that love is all about putting your personal comfort or best interest aside in order to best serve someone else.

There is even a movement within our own churches that is a subtle threat to the biblical way of living an others-focused lifestyle. It's subtle, but potentially harmful. New, MTV-type church services are popping up all over the country. These worship services are loud, colorful, hip, and drawing tons and tons of young people—which is a *good* thing. I am in no way opposed to filling the seats of those services! In fact, we have such a service close to where I serve, and some of our teenagers enjoy worshiping there on Sunday evenings.

Here's the danger though, some folks are starting to behave as though church is all about feeling and emotion. They become addicted to the buzz of feeling really good. This can happen in the context of a powerful "worship service," the buzz of the latest and greatest new devotional fad or book, it can look like a million different things. The danger is that Christianity becomes a self-focused lifestyle. We begin to measure our growth by our own personal experiences, our own time of being "caught in the moment" in worship. Soon, it becomes all about us.

Please understand that worship is a hugely important part of your growth as a disciple of Jesus Christ, but it mustn't stay there. It's important that we balance it with living for others, serving others. It's not just about going to some hip worship service and leave feeling really good. It's about loving others in a biblical way. It's about sharing the love of Christ, not hoarding it. It's worth mentioning "knowledge constipation" again here, when you build yourself up and fill yourself up with all sorts of new knowledge and experiences but never do anything to release it into the lives of other people. That is a threat to Christianity in the United States today. The idea that it's all about me, my personal growth, and feeling good about myself. I don't believe that it's a healthy perspective, though it is becoming more and more popular in our churches.

This past Christmas, I took thirteen teenagers with me and another adult to New York City for a leadership experience with the School of Urban Studies. During the experience, we were able to serve with Metro Ministries, the largest Sunday school program in the country. For most of our teenagers, it started out as just a fun experience. For them, the whole point of it was simply to have fun. Teenagers usually measure the value of an experience by how much fun it is; we intentionally try to shatter that way of thinking.

As the morning progressed, something started to happen. Our students slowly and painfully began to realize that there were little kids among them in desperate situations. Some of us were able to tag along with the buses that transported the kids to and from their homes. The stories that our teenagers heard on those buses, the things they saw, the way the children told tales of tragedy in their lives as though they were normal—because to them they were normal—began to break our teenagers. They began to see that the world doesn't revolve around their comfort. They began to realize that there are real stories out there of people living with real pain and need.

I believe that it's imperative for us as parents to teach our students how to think about people other than themselves and to act sacrificially for the sake of others. There are many ways to do this, big and small. You can do so through paradigm shifting experiences by using a little creativity and through teaching them how to sacrifice in little ways throughout the day.

Most of our teenagers have jobs these days. I think that's a good thing. What's bad is that most of our teenagers spend all of the money they earn on themselves. They buy the latest and greatest cell phone, video game system, clothes, jewelry...ad nauseam. Teach your teenager how to spend their money on things that will last forever. Here are some ideas to get you thinking:

- Teach them the importance of supporting your local church with your own personal money.

- Help them create a "love slush fund" that they can use to build up and encourage fellow Christian friends. For instance, if they participate in a student ministry, encourage them to use this fund to help pay the way for someone in their group to attend a mission trip or student activity that they might not otherwise be able to afford. Be sure to teach your teenager the value and joy of doing this anonymously.

- Help them create what Lee Yih, a missionary at Harvard University, calls a "mischief fund." Lee says that evangelism is actually "Christian mischief." In every conversation with a nonbeliever, you're actually scheming and plotting for a way to introduce them to Christ. You have an agenda...it's Christian mischief. I love that definition, and I believe it's very accurate. A "mischief fund" is simply money set aside and only used for those friends who don't know Christ.

It's used on things that will give the mischievous one an opportunity to share Christ with them. For example, your teenager could use it to take a friend out for lunch and have a strategy to share Christ during the meal. It could be used to pay for a non-Christian friend to attend a church outreach event, or maybe to buy their friend a gift they've always wanted to soften their friend's heart to the message.

The point is to somehow attach the gift to Jesus. If I buy my friend a video game that he can't afford, I'm going to say something like, "You know, I just feel that God has been so gracious and generous to me. I love sharing his goodness with other people." Then I would go into a specific story about how God's been good to me (there are about a million of these stories a day if you're paying attention).

It's also important for you to model and teach your teenager to live others-focused in small things, not just the big stuff. For instance, it's family movie day and everyone wants to see the latest teen-cult movie except for you. Instead of arguing or whining about how you are being dragged to this stupid movie, graciously put your own taste and comfort aside and watch the movie with your family. If you're staying at a motel and there are two beds and one cot and someone has to sleep on the floor, get over the fact that you're three times older than your teenager and sleep on the floor. You should model a servant lifestyle if you expect your teenagers to live it.

Teach your teenager that when it comes to living a servant lifestyle, your personal tastes and comforts are irrelevant. The only concern is doing what's best for the person you are serving, period.

Creating a Positive Family Dynamic

I believe that parents waste a lot of time nit picking their teenagers. Do any of these statements sound familiar?

"Sit up straight."

"Tuck your shirt in."

"Did you finish your homework yet?"

"Turn that music down."

"Don't sit so close to the television."

Man, oh man, it's giving me a headache just thinking about it. There are about a million things more important and productive to do than nit picking your kid to death. Instead of majoring on the minors, why not help them to live a compelling and fulfilling life? A life marked by a deep seeded maturity. The problem is, if you're always nagging on your teenager about minor, external issues, you lose your relational capital with her for the big stuff, the stuff that really matters. Things like helping them develop work ethic, integrity, authenticity, a passion for ministry...and about a million other important characteristics. Remember, the most important thing for you to do if you hope to raise a healthy, mature young person is to do whatever it takes to make sure that he or she feels accepted and unconditionally loved. If you nag your teens to death, it's telling them that they're never quite good enough, or that they're not one hundred percent acceptable in your eyes.

Rather than having ninety-eight things that you bug them about every day, decide on the few things that are unacceptable under your roof and only go to the wall for those things. Your list might include murder one, drugs, disrespecting their mother...really, there aren't a whole lot...most things are actually small things in the big picture. This will free you up to spend your energy and resources giving them a compelling vision for their lives rather than a list of petty no-nos.

In this section of the book, I will do two things:

- Help you establish a family mission and value system if you've not already done so.

- Develop a goal-oriented strategy for creating a mature and godly young adult (this part is my favorite!).

Establishing a Family Mission and Value System

Most families live without intentionality. They've never spent any time thinking about what kind of relationships they want to foster, what they want their home to "feel" like when friends and family walk through the front door, or what type of people they hope to nurture within their family system.

I can't overemphasize how important it is to be intentional with these things. You must spend time thinking and praying. You must have long conversations. You must put the effort forth to not only create and write a family mission and set of values, you must ruthlessly pursue real-life alignment with those values. If you simply write it down and stick it to your refrigerator door for everyone to see, you've missed the point. The key is to align your actions, words, and thoughts with the words you put on paper.

Let's start with getting the words on paper. I believe it's important that everyone in the family is involved in this process, as it increases the level of ownership. Be careful to not just "spring this" on your teenagers. You must be strategic about when and where to start the conversation about creating a family mission, or you'll likely be facing a negative, sarcastic, and cynical bunch. The best context in starting the discussion is while you are all having a blast together. Whether you're at your favorite restaurant, on family vacation, playing Scrabble...whatever, the point is to not allow it to become an overly formal and rigid activity. I think you'd be shooting yourself in the foot if you set this book down right now and announced, "Okay, troops, today we're making a family mission statement." They'd probably vote for a book-burning session, starting with this book. Be careful and strategic in how you introduce this concept to the family, but do emphasize that their involvement is important. Share with them why this is so important to you; they'll respect your honesty and efforts.

Like I said, I'm not big on "programming" this part of the process or having you go through a rigid series of questions. To me it's more of an intuitive process. It happens through conversation, deep thought, and reflection. Here are two important guidelines to keep in mind as you write your family values:

> 1. Write it in present tense. Write them as though they are already true.

> 2. Your values are something to shoot for. They are idealistic statements. They are a description of how your family operates in a perfect world. Thus, they should stretch you. If you read them before you start the day, it should give you something to work toward. If you read them at the end of the day, you

should be able to name the things that you did outside of your values and work on ways to improve on your actions and use of time.

Let's get started. Here are some questions to think through to get you thinking in the right direction, and then I'll give you our family's values as an example.

- When people come to your house for dinner, what do you want them to say in the car ride on the way home about your home environment?

- What do you want them to say about the way you interacted with each other?

- What do you wish would have been different about your family life growing up?

- What do you appreciate most about your family life growing up?

Here are our family's values. You'll notice that I give a core statement and then a brief summary that serves to "flesh out" the concept.

We are Relationship Centered

We use things for people, not people for things. We don't see each other as interruptions to our "to-do" lists. We see relationships as the most important thing on earth. We laugh, cry, and celebrate together. We accept each other, as evident in the way we treat each other. We actively, intentionally, and whole-heartedly support one another. We resolve conflict immediately and completely. We actively listen to one another. We negotiate and compromise, always looking for the win-win solution. We do what's best for the other.

We Have an Organized and Neat Home Environment

We put things away right away. Everything has its place. We all participate in managing and maintaining the home environment and systems. We detest clutter. We believe that an organized and neat home environment maximizes productivity, peace, and joy in the lives of those who live there.

We Have an Eternal Perspective

We are a bridge for people to build upon or enter into a relationship with Jesus Christ. We aim to build up eternal treasures, not earthly treasures. We see everything we own as a tool rather than an idol. We use our talents, resources, finances, and energy for eternal things. Our highest aim is to honor God with our lives and serve him wholeheartedly.

Whatever values you choose, they have to be specific to your family and agreed upon by everyone. Ownership is obviously very important. Take the time to think and pray carefully about this, as it has huge implications for the legacy that you will pass on to your teenagers on what a healthy family looks, feels, and acts like.

Aligning Your Actions with the Family Values

Fortune-500 companies pay big bucks for consultants to give their employees a weekend retreat, where they spend hours talking about and creating company mission statements and values. Then comes Monday morning, and people forget what they wrote. Most companies have no strategy for aligning their everyday actions with the company's mission statement or values. Perhaps the mission statement and values are on a banner in the conference room, or even on the company letterhead, but their actions display no evidence of alignment. Thus, thousands and thousands of dollars were wasted in creating these valuable statements, because they never did anything with them.

The same thing will happen with your family values if you don't create a strategy for aligning your family atmosphere and actions with them. Here are some suggestions for helping you honor the time you spent creating your values by actually living them out. Don't underestimate the importance of this exercise!

1. Teach your teenagers and discuss at least once a month the importance of choosing their actions rather than reacting. Steven Covey describes it as the space between stimulus and response. That space is occupied by our free will. Simply put, something happens to you, and you have the power to choose how to respond in the space between what happens to you and your next action. You don't have to have a knee-jerk reaction. We as humans are afforded the luxury to choose how we will respond. That space in the middle, which is occupied by free will, is where your values and mission come into play. Here are two questions that you should always ask yourself before any action, word or thought:

   • Is this going to help me become more like the person I want to become? (This statement has everything to do with your mission and values.)

- Is this going to help me accomplish the things in life that I want to accomplish? (This statement has everything to do with your goals, which we will tackle in a few moments.)

Of course, this is also where you teach your family how to moment by moment depend on the Holy Spirit. Teach them how to say one-liner prayers to God throughout the day. Remember, your prayers don't have to start with "Dear Heavenly Father..." This is a perfectly wonderful prayer, "God, I'm not sure what my next action should be, please help me do the right thing." The more you are able to convince your teens the importance of moment-to-moment dependence on God, the better.

2. Another way to help your family align your actions with your values is to have a weekly fifteen minute refresher meeting. Notice that I said fifteen minutes. If you tenaciously guard the time frame, not going any longer than fifteen minutes, it won't be such a drag for your teenagers, and it will be easier to keep it as a consistent weekly appointment. Remember, it's better to end the meeting with them wanting more than ending it after they've been mentally and emotionally checked out for the past thirty minutes.

These weekly meetings should consist of one person reading the core statement and description of one of your family values, and then everyone should participate in answering three questions:

- Where are we doing really well as a family in this area?

- Where are we dropping the ball as a family in this area?

- What are we going to do differently this week?

3. Publicly and specifically praise someone in your family when they act consistently with one of your values.

"Abby, I am so proud of the way you didn't get upset with your brother when he broke your iPod. You knew it was just an accident and that he felt terrible. By you being gentle, forgiving, and tender toward him, it reinforces our family value of relationships being first; people are more important than things. Your mother and I have decided to buy you a new iPod based on your gracious response."

All right, folks, it's your turn. I suggest that you set aside some time with your family to have the discussions and agree on several family values then creatively make space in your schedules for consistent time together to flesh out how to live out your chosen family values. In creating your values together, write as many of the values out on paper as you can think of and then begin to narrow the list down to some core values. It's okay to write for the trash can the first time around, it's a rough draft. Just get something in writing, give everyone a copy, and have them think and pray about it. They can make notes of anything they'd like to add, remove, or change, and then revisit the statements in a week to improve or tweak your values. Then you are ready to start the alignment process. Have fun!

Developing Mature and Godly Young Adults

I want you to picture something in your mind's eye. Make it vivid, realistic. Include as many details in this imagined scene as possible. It's your son or daughter's high school graduation. Picture what they will look like with the cap and gown. Smell the gym or the outdoors. See all your friends and loved ones there with you cheering for your high school graduate! See the people taking pictures, the sea of navy blue or black caps and gowns. Hear the commencement speaker giving his "good luck in the real world" speech. Hear your son or daughter's name called as they receive their diploma.

It's a very important day, a day that stirs up a lot of emotions for parents. The question is, are they ready? At this point, it's too late to start being intentional about parenting. You've either prepared them for the real world or you haven't.

On that day, what type of values do you want them to have? What type of character will they have? Are they disciplined and hard-working? Are they confident in who God has made them, or timid and self-defeating? Do they have a passion and enthusiasm for living, or do they just wade aimlessly through life? Are they resilient, or fragile? Do they have a sense of entitlement or humility?

Here is where the hard work of parenting really happens.

You are responsible for raising mature adults. In order to do this, you need to begin with the end in mind. You need to have a vision for what you want your son or daughter to look like upon graduating from high school...or you could leave it up to society, school, friends, teachers, coaches, and bosses to shape and mold your kid...not a good idea.

Too many of our teenagers in church can spout off a million verses from memory, give all the right "Sunday school answers," and pray like a saint in front of the class without it really affecting their lives. They measure their "spirituality" by their knowledge of the Word and spiritual etiquette. Then they're jerks to their parents and friends, they never get up when the alarm goes off, and their room is a mess... yaddah yaddah. What a shame that we as a church sometimes give them the impression that as long as they have Psalm 23 memorized, the rest of their life doesn't matter. We need more Christian teenagers who get up when the alarm goes off and make their beds in the morning. We need more teenagers who can communicate with confidence when they meet someone new. We need teenagers who enjoy reading and writing. We need more "mature" Christian teenagers.

This conversation is for you and your spouse, no teenagers. Sit down with some coffee and a journal. Start planning out what your teenagers will look like when they graduate from high school. Write out a "goal character trait" for each character trait that you choose to intentionally develop in your teenager. For instance, you might have "Resilient" as a goal character trait. Design a strategy to foster that character trait in the life of your teenager by writing the answers to the following questions in the pages of your journal (I suggest two pages per characteristic):

Goal Character Trait

- What attitudes in my teenager must be changed or avoided?

- What steps can we take to encourage this characteristic?

- Things to watch in our own attitude or actions:

- How can we positively and intentionally model this characteristic?

- How should we be praying specifically for this area?

This will take time and energy, and obviously you shouldn't tackle your entire list of goals at once. Start by brainstorming all the characteristics you'd like to see in your child, and then decide together where to start. I would focus on one characteristic per month. As you begin to build these characteristics into the life of your teenager, set aside time, once a month, to systematically review and reprocess your goal sheets. Here's a sample of what a typical goal sheet might look like:

Goal Character Trait: *Creativity*

- What attitudes in my teenager must be changed or avoided? *Laziness when it comes to reading and learning. Boredom by lack of adventure and stimulation by trying new things in life. Thinking that adventure is sitting in front of a screen, watching mindless television. Living everyday life with a "same old, same old" mentality. Not being open to new and challenging experiences.*

- What steps can we take to encourage this characteristic? *Put a sledgehammer through the television. Have a video-game-system-burning party. Hike the Appalachian Trail with her this summer. Start a family book club. Have her write out a list of one hundred things that she wants to do before she dies then start plotting with her how to accomplish them. Take her to the orchestra. Expose her to new experiences as frequently as possible. Teach her to think new thoughts instead of recycling the same old thoughts every day.*

- Things to watch in our own attitude or actions: *Mental laziness. The tendency to rather watch TV than read. Boring dinner conversation rather than stimulating conversation. Lack of new experiences. Cynicism or sarcasm when our daughter shares her dreams and passions. Lack of drive to live adventurous lives, thinking that it takes too much planning and effort.*

- How can we positively and intentionally model this characteristic? *Plan a family adventure. Make a goal of reading at least three books per month, including books that are normally out of our mental comfort zone. Be intentional about planning family outings in which we are trying new things, such as mountain biking, white water rafting, rock climbing, hunting, weekend trips to New York City, mini family mission trips, skiing in Colorado, etc.*

- How should we be praying specifically for this area? *That our teenager wouldn't develop creativity for the sake of creativity. That it would awaken her to new levels of passionate living, expanding her perception of God. That creativity would bleed into everything she does, including thinking of new ways to attract non-believers to a compelling life in Christ. That she would break the "same old, same old" mold found in so many churches today, expanding her ministry influence within her own sphere of friends.*

Here's a list of characteristics that you might consider. This is not an exhaustive list, just some things that I think are important. Read it carefully, considering where your teenager compares to the ideal description of each characteristic, and then make goals accordingly.

The List

He Has Endurance

He has the ability to hold up under fire. He doesn't fold when things get difficult or mundane. Long after everyone else has forgotten the reason for setting a certain course of action, he remembers. He has a tenacious ability and drive to finish what he has started. He believes that the size of a person is determined by how much or how little it takes to stop him, and it requires large amounts to stop him, thus he has a life that most only dream of. When he sets goals or says he's going to do something, you might as well consider it done.

She is Committed

I heard "Prof" Howard Hendricks once say that if someone wants to change the world they need to be committed to three things:

1- God. 2- His Word. 3- Reaching the world. She is deeply committed to all three, setting aside her time, energy, resources, and money for eternal purposes.

He is a Thinker
He always has a list of things that he's thinking through. He uses paper to work through his thoughts. He has a "thinking journal," which is filled with mind maps, ideas, charts, sketches, and decision trees. He is always figuring out ways to think better, to think more positively, to think more effectively and to think more Biblically.

She is a Reader
She reads widely and deeply. She has a passion for reading the Bible, as well as old Christian classics. She keeps up with world news by reading newspapers and magazines. She has several magazine subscriptions and reads books of all types. She always has a book near and finishes a book almost every week. She has a system for highlighting and noting the book she is currently reading, and a system for processing and reviewing books she has already read.

He is Pure in Heart
He doesn't sacrifice his intimacy with God, or his fulfillment in life, with fleeting moments of passion. He has a list of activities to do and people to call when he is experiencing intense temptation. He has trained himself to bounce his eyes from images that bombard him on a daily basis. He immediately and completely

replaces impure thoughts in his head with things that are positive, praiseworthy, and pure. He is completely dependent on God every moment of his life to keep him pure and holy in his thoughts, words, and actions.

She is a Problem Solver

She knows how to change a flat tire, check the oil, and use jumper cables. She doesn't get flustered when she runs into obstacles; she calmly thinks through her options and then acts in the most appropriate manner. She is proactive about solving her personal issues and sees her ability to tackle issues immediately and effectively as one of her greatest assets, because it is. She has mentally rehearsed her response to every possible situation, from her firm response to someone asking her if she wants to take drugs, to her aggressive response to a man approaching her alone in a parking lot. She's a survivor.

He is Creative

He understands that the more creative he is in life, the more impact he will have in whatever he sets his mind to. He has an insatiable curiosity, from wanting to understand the way an engine works to wanting to understand the way a woman's mind works. He is always thinking up new ways to do things. He keeps a dream journal and is continually adding things to his "Do Before I Die" list. He understands that the God he serves is not boring and thus he refuses to lead a boring life. He is adventurous and creative in all things, big and small. It's a way of life for him. He's always exposing himself to new and creative concepts and people. He hates TV; while his friends are all watching reality TV, he's out there living it.

She is Disciplined
She wakes up early in the morning and makes her bed. She does what she is supposed to do in the best possible manner at the time she is supposed to do it. She is not led or swayed by feelings, moods, or emotions. She executes.

He is Grateful
He does not have a sense of entitlement, he is thankful for what he has. He doesn't give the waitress a hard time or return his food if it's slightly cold. He simply thanks God for the blessing of having a meal to begin with and says not a word. He has a healthy perspective of how fortunate he is to live in this time and place.

She is Polite
She says "please" and "thank you" and looks in your eye when she shakes your hand. She uses proper table etiquette and thanks you for the wonderful meal. She is always looking for ways to make the people around her feel comfortable, accepted, and loved. She thinks of others more highly than herself.

He is a Goal Setter
He knows the importance of setting powerful and inspiring goals. Most of his goals are aimed at his own spiritual growth and helping others grow in their walk with Christ.

He focuses on things like helping his friend develop a consistent prayer time by praying with him until it becomes a habit; having a hard conversation with a friend who is picking up some bad habits; starting a Scripture-memory program with his sister. He also has goals that will inspire creativity and passion in his own walk, like hiking the Rocky Mountains with his accountability group, and developing his mountain biking skills in order to spend more time with some of his non-Christian friends who enjoy riding a good trail. He is intentional with his time and knows how to move consistently and strategically toward the accomplishment of his goals. Because of his sense of purpose that comes from setting goals, he is able to say "no" to things that sidetrack him, and he does so without feeling guilty. Because of his goal system, he has a healthy sense of accomplishment, achievement, dependence on God, and gratefulness.

She is a Thermostat

She is not a thermometer, which merely measures the temperature of a room. She is a thermostat, she determines the temperature of a room. When she walks into a conversation among her friends, she raises the temperature of that conversation. She raises the bar. Coarse language stops out of respect. Gossip stops because her friends know it will be confronted. When she walks into a room, the bar raises.

He Has a Strong Work Ethic

He is known among his friends as a hard worker. He appreciates the value of hard work, both physically and mentally. He is able to sustain long periods of concentrated work ethic without ever complaining or feeling sorry for himself. In fact, he seems to enjoy it. He enjoys everything from chopping and stacking wood to studying for a difficult school exam. He takes simple pleasure in his work, whatever kind it may be.

She Has a Well-guarded Private Life

She understands the model of Jesus' healthy balance of public ministry and private isolation. She knows that a strong person in public is a stronger person in private. She has a consistent daily time for reflection and thinking, a monthly time of three to five hours for thinking, praying, and planning and an annual one- or two-day period of solitude for journaling, praying, and asking God for direction in her life. She guards her quiet times as though her life depends on them.

He Has a Healthy Sense of Confidence

He believes that his parents believe that he can do anything. He knows that his confidence is not in himself, but in Christ, who lives in him, and the ability that God has given him. He confidently shares his God-given gifts with the world around him. He doesn't speak words of false humility; he thanks people when they complement him, gently reflecting the glory back to God for giving him the ability. He understands that his identity is in no way attached to his achievement, and because of that he feels no pressure to achieve; thus, he consistently performs at a higher level than his friends who feel the pressure to succeed. He is not afraid of failure, he sees it as an opportunity to learn.

She is Resilient

She understands that the world will throw her curveballs every now and again. She doesn't get angry, frustrated, or emotional when things don't go exactly as planned. She is able to change course or make adjustments without getting emotionally overwhelmed. She takes things in stride and is never overwhelmed by her circumstances, no matter how difficult or adverse they may be.

He is Authentic

He is completely comfortable in his own skin. He acknowledges his weaknesses, but doesn't dwell on them. He doesn't hide his motives or intentions. He shoots straight from the hip, graciously but honestly. He is the same person wherever he is, whomever he's with.

She Handles Conflict Well

She deals with uncomfortable tension in relationships immediately. She goes through life with no emotional or relational baggage, handling misunderstandings and miscommunications as soon as they occur. She doesn't "vent" to others; rather she sincerely asks for input on how to handle difficult situations. She goes directly to the person with whom she has conflict and talks it through face to face. Sometimes she writes her thoughts out on paper first so that she doesn't allow emotions of the moment to cloud her thoughts and judgment, but she always handles these situations face to face.

He Lives with Excellence

Whatever he does, he does it the best he knows. He doesn't half-heart anything. If he works at McDonald's, he gradually moves his way up the ladder for his great attitude and his ability to always do the chores that nobody else likes to do, and he does so with passion and great care. If he is studying for a test, he takes strategic brain breaks but is intensely focused during the periods of study. With his power of concentration, he is able to accomplish twice as much in half the time that the typical teenager spends on homework. He also pursues excellence in his relationships. He has open and authentic conversations with his parents every evening, and his kid sister loves him for teaching her how to throw a football. He cares about things that most teenagers don't care about. He lives with excellence.

She is Intentional about Creating Positive Life Habits

She understands that most of her everyday life is determined by ingrained habits, so she's intentional about developing habits that will help her to be the person she wants to become and succeed at doing the things she wants to accomplish with her life. She forms a new life-enhancing habit every ninety days, which is realistically how long it takes her to establish a new habit. She knows that her success in life will be determined by her ability to be self-controlled and intentional with the minor, everyday actions of life, which add up to a lifetime.

He is a Great Conversationalist

People think of him as a great conversationalist because he knows how to ask great questions, and he listens to you as though you're the only other person on earth. He searches out what you're interested in during the conversation and rarely spends any time thinking about what he's going to say when you're done talking. He just listens deeply. He is truly interested in learning everything he can about everyone he can. When you are talking with him, you feel understood, respected, and admired.

She is Teachable

She doesn't have a "know-it-all" attitude. She understands that she doesn't have the life experience of most people. She asks for advice and has a list of people that she wants to be influenced by.

He Has a Large Capacity for Believing God

There are things in his life that he is trying to accomplish that he knows would be impossible for him to accomplish under his own strength. He knows that the size of his effectiveness in life and ministry is determined by the size of his God. He knows that God delights in using people who are fully devoted and fully dependent on God in big ways. He is comfortable living in the unknown, trusting in God's provision.

Prodigals–If It Seems too Late…

Much of my college years were spent as far away from God as possible. I didn't like church; for the most part I thought it was boring. I enjoyed sinning because it was immediate gratification, and frankly it was a lot of fun…for the moment, but somewhere deep in me, there was this strange pain. It was the pain of emptiness. The pain of absence. It took me several years to realize what was absent from my life—God.

To their credit, my parents never forced me to go to church. They never shamed me for not wanting to go to youth group. It was my choice, and I chose not to go.

I think that if they would have put me on a guilt trip or forced me to join a youth group, I would have built up a deep resentment against them *and* church. I would have seen it as a chore. I would have hated every second of it.

I remember when I was in high school, the youth pastor of the church I attended on Sunday mornings and his friend took me and my best friend to a Cleveland Cavs basketball game. I remember it vividly; the seats were great, so was the company. My best friend and I were treated like kings that night. At first I was a bit apprehensive about going because I thought they would talk to us about going to youth group. They didn't. In fact, church never even came up. They asked us questions about our lives, our dreams. They affirmed us, appreciated us. They listened. They didn't lecture, they listened. By the end of the evening, I was convinced that they actually cared about my life.

I'll never forget that trip to the old coliseum. Never. I am grateful to this day for their example. If you've never experienced real ministry, if you don't know what it looks like, reread the previous paragraph. That, my friends, is ministry.

Too many parents act out of desperation and fear rather than trust. It comes down to trusting the sovereignty of God. Do you trust that God is good? Do you trust that God is in control? If you can say yes to both of those questions, you can live in peace. You must trust your child in God's hands.

Let that sit with you for a while.

You must trust your child in God's hands.

The more you push, the more you try to force religion onto your child, the farther you are pushing them from an authentic and meaningful relationship with Christ. Think about it; if you're child is not a Christian, what good is it to force your beliefs on him? It doesn't work. You must ask yourself the question, *Am I more interested in changing his behavior or having God change his heart?* Without the Holy Spirit active in his life, of course he's not going to hunger and thirst after righteousness. The Holy Spirit is the one who gives us not only the power but also the desire to become more like Jesus. Helping him find Jesus should be your highest aim, not helping him "act" more like a Christian.

It seems counterintuitive, but the best thing that you can do is to release your teenager to God. What I mean by that is to simply stop seeing it as your personal mission to force your kid into a relationship with Jesus Christ.

Start a Prayer Group

One of the most powerful ministries I know of is a group of parents who regularly get together to share their struggles with each other and pray together about their prodigal children. It is a tremendously encouraging ministry for those parents who think they might be the only ones out there. You would be surprised at how many parents are heartbroken over the same things that you are.

This is also one of the most effective types of prayer meetings, because the prayers are raw and unedited. People pray with grief, anger, frustration, resentment, sadness, and a sense of hopelessness. Because of the perceived desperation of their situations, they don't pray medicated prayers that we are so used to hearing in church. Once you turn something over to God, the impossible becomes possible. The unlikely becomes probable. The most difficult situation becomes an opportunity for God to show himself strong. He likes to do that, and he will. Trust him. Lay your burdens at his feet. Allow him to do the heavy lifting; it's too much for you to bear. God is the only one strong enough, powerful enough to change the inner-workings of a human heart. Leave it to him.

Let God Be Their Savior, Not Mom

Nancy Leigh DeMoss said something that I'll never forget, "Don't rescue your child from the cross." Easy to say, gut-wrenchingly difficult to do.

God has his own ways of reaching us when we reject him or wander. It's true that sometimes he brings us to a low point in our lives. For me it was my fourth year of college.

I was a good basketball player in high school, very good. I received all kinds of awards and recognition. I didn't feel that I needed God, because I felt that I *was* god, and Friday nights in the Wooster High School gym was my congregation. That is painfully shameful to say, but that's how I felt. I thought I could do anything. My senior year, I felt that we could beat any high school basketball team in the country,

I truly believed that. In fact, we defeated Saginaw Buena Vista High School in a holiday tournament. They were a team loaded with all-stars. They were ranked the fourth best team in the nation according to *USA Today* and had a fifty-seven game win-streak—not after we beat them. Guess who got tournament MVP honors?

I felt invincible. I received a full scholarship to play basketball at Valparaiso University, and I was part of what was hailed as the best freshmen class in the school's history. Enter God.

Slowly, but surely, God began to strip me of my confidence. Remember, basketball was an idol of sorts for me. It was my identity.

It started with my final high school game; it was a tournament game against our league rival. They completely rattled me, it was the worst game of my high school career. Sitting in direct eye line as I watched the final moments of the game was my new college coach. I was confused and angry with my performance, and my confidence began to decay.

The downward spiral continued with my first college open gym. I played terribly, maybe the worst I've ever played, and I never recovered. I experienced something that I had never before experienced in my basketball life. I got depressed, angry, and insecure. As the team was experiencing amazing success, playing in the NCAA Division 1 tournament twice, I found myself more and more distancing myself from my teammates. I couldn't stand the celebrations, I didn't understand why I was losing my abilities. By sheer force of will, I had a brief period of success in the pre-season open gyms of my sophomore year, but it soon fell apart again. After three years at Valparaiso, I decided to transfer to a small college in Michigan.

My new school had a less than great basketball program. After the worst season record of any team that I had ever played on since fifth grade, I was angry. I was looking for other things to medicate the anger, nothing worked.

I was sitting alone in my dorm room, flipping through the channels on TV. To my chagrin, Valparaiso University was experiencing national success in the NCAA tournament; they had won their first two games of the NCAA tournament and were set to play in the Sweet Sixteen. They had become the Cinderella team, the nation's darlings. As I flipped through the channels, every single channel available on my TV had something about Valparaiso. They were either interviewing my old teammates, showing highlights of their games, or talking about possibilities of a Final Four appearance. I was sick to my stomach.

Finally, I turned it to *The David Letterman Show*. I figured I would be safe there from having to hear anything about my former team's success. Little did I know that David Letterman is actually from Indiana. To my horror, he applauded the success of the Valparaiso Crusaders on his national late-night television show.

I lost it. It was literally the lowest point of my life. Everything that I had ever put my hope in, every dream that I ever dreamed was happening...to my former teammates, and I was alone in my dorm room at a little college in southern Michigan.

In a fit of rage and sorrow, I slammed my remote control against the wall, fell to my knees on the floor, and screamed at God, "How could you do this to me? You know that basketball is the most important thing in my life!"

My outburst was followed by a deafening silence; it was God giving me space to consider the implications of my words. I went from my knees to my face on the ground.

"I'm sick of this pain. I don't know where to go or what to do. I don't know what it looks like to be a real Christian, but if you'll show me, if you'll get me away from this misery of never being satisfied, I'll follow you with everything I have." What followed was a subjective feeling of peace like

I had never experienced. From that point on, God began to put people in my life who discipled, mentored, and graciously walked with me as I began to figure out what it meant to follow the one whose name we bear. That peace has never left me.

If your teenager is searching for that peace, trying to find fulfillment in everything but God, you might just have to leave them to their devices. If they cringe, kick, and rebel when you talk with them about God, you're not helping. They need to have a sense of deep need for God before they are able to completely surrender to him. If they don't feel a need for God, nothing you repeatedly say is going to convince them; it will only deepen their resolve to find another way. Don't rescue them from the desperate situation in which God might put them in order to get their attention.

Your best course of action is to spend more time than you can afford on your knees in prayer. Pray often and long for your child. Love them until they ask why. Be gracious and gentle. Love them to God, don't push them.

Now, if your teenager is already a Christian, you're playing by a different set of rules. If your teenager has authentically turned their life over to Christ and their salvation is secure, then you have every reason and responsibility to rebuke and warn them when they are living in rebellion. Remember, this must *not* be a personal taste issue for you. If it's something that just annoys you, learn to live with it. If it's something big, something that is truly an act of rebellion against God, something that you have decided is worth going to the wall for, then you must speak up.

Psalm 32:9 is a powerful verse that illustrates the painful way that God sometimes gets our attention through difficult or desperate situations,

> Be not like a horse or a mule, without understanding, which must be curbed with bit and bridle, or it will not stay near you.

In other words, don't be like a mule that is unruly, where God has to sometimes painfully and violently jerk the bit in your mouth in order to get you on the right path. I remember talking to a teenager who was living in serious rebellion and coldness toward God. I pulled her aside one day after our Sunday morning lesson, shared Psalm 32:8–9 with her, and gave her some stern, but loving, advice.

"Young lady, I'm going to tell you something, but I want you to understand that I'm telling you this because I'm concerned for you. It's not out of malice, it's not a scare tactic, it's simply a heads-up for what's about to happen to you. You are living in intentional opposition to God right now. Your heart is becoming harder each moment you continue to live this way, and you must repent. You must change. You must get back on the right path. We're all here for you, and we love you more than you know right now. We will help in any way that we can, and God will immediately and completely forgive you when you turn back to him, but you must do so swiftly. If you choose to continue taking this alternate path, God will do something to get your attention. It will be painful, like the jerking of a mule's head to get him back on the right path. Let God correct you gently. Soften your heart to him. The harder and longer you rebel, the more painful it will be for God to get your attention."

It may seem a bit dramatic, but I needed to get her attention. Your job is to give them the warning, then leave them to God.

Most importantly, be encouraged. If your son or daughter is living apart from God, take heart that it's not your responsibility to bring them back to God. That's what he does best. Leave it to him. Replace your worry and nagging with prayer. Pray long and hard, it works. I've seen miracle after miracle of God restoring someone to an intimate and powerful relationship with him, while people behind the scenes are wearing out their knees in prayer. He loves to show himself strong on behalf of those who fully trust and depend on him.

Remember the two pillars of our faith:

- God is good.
- God is in control.

Believe that.

Some Final Words

I was sitting with my wife at a beautiful resort, listening to Dr. Howard Hendricks and Dr. Michael Easley give advice on how to have a successful marriage, and they said something that has really stuck with me. It's something that I'm growing in to. It's Prof. Hendricks secret to a healthy marriage: *focus on their strengths*.

It is easy for parents to get into the habit of dwelling on the negatives. If you wanted to, you could probably make a list of one hundred things that your teenagers do every day that you would consider annoying or negative. We could do the same thing with our spouses, but that is no way to live.

When sin entered the world, it warped our thinking in many ways, one of those ways is that we now have a natural bend toward negativity. I'll prove it to you. Say you're meeting with your boss for the end-of-the-year review. He gives you a list of all the positive things you've done for the company and all the positive characteristics he appreciates about you. Then he shares with you two things that he sees as negative, things that you need to work on. You will naturally spend the rest of that day and evening thinking about and being anxious or frustrated about the two negatives that he mentioned. You will have forgotten all about the lists of positives he gave you.

If we're not intentional as parents or spouses about how

we think about our teenagers (or spouse), we will allow our focus to gravitate toward the negative. Gradually, our perception of our teenager will be that of frustration, only seeing the negatives. We must have a plan for not only seeing the positives in our teenagers' lives and personalities, we must also set them up for success by helping them to dwell on and maximize their God-given gifts and positive attributes.

Focusing on Their Positives

My first Sunday serving at my current church was quite interesting. I had inherited a group of students who had a lot of energy, and some ornery ones at that. As I was teaching my first Sunday school class, one of them began to act up. He was testing his new boundaries with his new youth director. I stopped right in the middle of my teaching and asked him to visit with me out in the hall. There were oohs and ahhs and people saying, "You're in trouble now." I just laughed.

As we talked in the hall, I asked him to look me in the eye. He was a lot different now that it was just us two. He was bracing for a stern scolding, but what he got surprised him, I affirmed him.

"Boy, I am impressed by you, my friend."

"Huh?"

"I've not seen someone with your spunk, creativity, and energy in a while." (I was being completely serious and honest.)

"What do you mean?" he said, surprised but grinning.

"Well, it's these kids. They're all watching you. I think you're the leader of this pack, is that right?"

"Yeah...I guess so."

"Well, you're a football player, I hear...so I'm going to coach you right now. Are you up for a challenge?"

"Sure, yeah."

"I want you to use that natural leadership ability and

charisma to help me build this ministry. I want you around at our events. I want you to follow me, and they will naturally follow you. God has given you some ability here, you can either use it to glorify him or use it to glorify yourself. You choose."

When we walked back into the classroom, everything changed. He began challenging people to pay attention when they started goofing off. He attended almost all of our programs and activities, and people followed—like I knew they would. He wasn't perfect and made mistakes, but he was one of the kids responsible for helping me start the ministry off on the right foot.

Did you catch what happened? Rather than focusing on the negatives, which would have been easy to do, I chose to affirm his strengths, which were his charisma and natural leadership abilities. We need to start thinking about the strengths we see in each other and figure out ways to help those around us better use them for the Kingdom of God.

Rather than scolding your teenager for not being able to sit still through church, affirm, appreciate, and encourage him for having so much energy and help him figure out how to spend that energy on healthy, productive things.

Rather than scolding your teenager for getting in trouble for drawing during history, affirm, appreciate, and encourage his passion for drawing by buying him a sketchbook and some charcoal pencils.

Rather than scolding your kid for not agreeing with you in a political conversation, affirm, appreciate, and encourage him for having strong opinions of his own.

Rather than scolding your kid for getting a C in biology, affirm, appreciate, and encourage him for his natural affinity for history, where he received an A.

Rather than scolding your football player son for getting a mandatory detention for fighting in school, affirm, appreciate, and encourage him for standing on a wall for the kid who always gets beat up by the school bully.

Focus on your teenagers' strengths. Appreciate their personality quirks rather than feeling you need to change them. Don't apologize to others for your kid. Don't be embarrassed by your kid. Don't compare your kid to anyone ever. Thank God for making him exactly the way that he made him.

Setting Your Teenagers Up for Success

Don't sabotage your teenager. You're goal is to set her up for success in life. It's the same thing with your spouse. Why on earth would you ask your wife to handle the checkbook if she's terrible with numbers? You're just setting her up for frustration and failure. It's the same thing with your teenager. Why on earth would you want him to be a doctor if he can't stand blood, or a lawyer if she hates debating with people. Your responsibility in this section is two-fold:

> 1. Help your teenagers discover their gifts, talents, and passions.

> 2. Encourage the daylights out of your teenagers to pursue those areas of gifting.

Helping Your Teenagers Discover Their Gifts, Talents, and Passions

This is the adventurous part of being a parent. Allow your teenagers to try any and everything they show any interest in. Too many parents have a plan for their teenager before they can even walk. Don't bring your baggage into this process; it's not about you living your dreams through your kid. That's unfair and immature. Your job is to help them discover *their* gifts and passions.

If you take your daughter to the ballet and you see her face light up, ask her if she'd like to take a six-week intro to ballet class. It shouldn't be a large commitment of time at first, just something long enough to get their feet wet to see if there's any real interest.

If your kid shows some ability and interest in art, take him to an art museum, a great one.

If your kid lights up when you take him to the baseball game, sign him up for little league.

Encourage your kid to try everything until she finds those things where she has some ability and passion. I think it's important that they're not just passionate but also have some natural ability. This is just a natural part in setting teenagers up for success.

My parents encouraged me to play basketball because I had some natural advantages and gifts (I am six feet seven inches tall and slender). I probably wouldn't have been a very good wrestler, so they just steered me away from going that direction. They kept me from doing something for which I just physically wasn't built. To me, that's smart parenting.

Give your teenagers some short-term experience in anything and everything they show interest in, without overcrowding their calendars. My personal conviction is that teenagers should only participate in one (or two) extracurricular activity at a time. Home life is too important to never have them around.

Encourage them to try...

- Fencing
- Piano
- Swimming
- Tennis
- Underwater Basket Weaving
- Basketball
- Writing
- Drawing
- Painting
- Lacrosse

- Sumo Wrestling
- Soccer
- Quiz team
- Debate team
- Chess club
- Electric guitar
- Rock climbing

Once they find their sweet spot, encourage them to pursue it. When a kid discovers that she has some ability in a certain activity, it builds confidence and self-esteem. That's a good thing. It will also develop in her certain important characteristics such as work ethic, discipline, goal setting, humility, etc.

Help Them Spend Their Talents on Eternal Things

Once they are actively pursuing their sweet spot, begin to help them have a vision of how to spend it on things that will last beyond their own lives. If they simply do an activity for their own glory or to feel good about themselves, they are missing out on an important lesson on stewardship.

Biblical stewardship is all about understanding that everything we have and everything we do is either an idol or a tool. A tool, biblically speaking, is something that you use for eternal benefits, not temporary. If your kid is a great swimmer, you should brainstorm with him ways that he could use that talent for eternal benefits.

Be creative here, let's stick to the swimming example and brainstorm some ideas of what that might look like.

- Pool passes are often expensive, so maybe he could raise some money from his friends to buy passes for little kids who might not otherwise be able to have any pool time.

- Help him see swimming as an act of worship. Watch "Chariots of Fire" with him and talk about the powerful quote spoken by Eric Liddell, which talks about his motivation for running: "I believe God made me for a purpose, but he also made me fast. And when I run, I feel his pleasure."
- Perhaps he could volunteer his time to teach inner-city kids the basic swim strokes and couple it with an evangelical Bible study.
- Perhaps he could organize a team Bible study for his high school swim team.
- Perhaps he could partner with his youth pastor to hold a swimming camp for the kids they meet on their next mission trip.

There are a million things that he could do. Help him to think creatively and have fun with it.

This parenting thing is no easy deal. It's something that we must take very seriously. We must be intentional. We must have a vision for our teenagers. We must study, read, talk, dream, plan, and pray. It's an adventure, and there isn't a "one-size-fits-all" plan. Each teenager is different, each parent is different.

Pick a few things that you've read in this book and create a plan to implement them into your "parenting toolbox." Don't try everything at once. Write those two or three things down and pray about them every night. Every morning when you wake up, write them down again on a sheet of paper until you've actually implemented them. This will keep you mindful of them. If you don't do anything with what you learn or become convicted about, it turns to vapor. In which case, this book was nothing more than an interesting read. Do something with it.

Mostly, enjoy the adventure, and pray like there's no tomorrow.

Endnotes

1 Krzyzewski, Mike. *Leading With the Heart*. New York: Warner. 2000. p. 10.

2 Milne, A.A. *The House at Pooh Corner*. New York: E.P. Dutton. 1961. p. 120.

3 I would encourage anyone and everyone reading this book to buy, study, read and live Dennis McCallum's book, *Walking in Victory*. Navpress. 1999. You will also find a wealth of wisdom on www.xenos.org, the website of the church where Dennis McCallum and Gary DeLashmutt serve as leaders and teachers. Their teachings have permanently marked my walk with Christ, my life.

4 Chart taken from Dennis McCallum, *Walking in Victory*, posted on www.xenos.org/essays/law-grc.htm.

5 Elias, Ph.D., Maurice J., Steven E. Tobias, Psy.D., Brian S. Friedlander, Ph.D. . *Emotionally Intelligent Parenting*. New York: Harmony Books. 1999. p. 61–2.

6   www.dictionary.com

7   McGraw, Dr. Phil. *Family First*. New York: Free
     Press. 2004. p. 156.

8   Cloud, Dr. Henry. *Integrity*. New York:
     HarperCollins. 2006.

9   Read more about this concept, as well as the
     lost art of conversation in Susan Scott's pow-
     erful book, *Fierce Conversations*. Susan Scott.
     Fierce Conversations. New York: The Berkley
     Publishing Group. 2002.

10   Carson, D.A. *For the Love of God*. Wheaton:
     Crossway Books. 1998.

11   Henry Cloud talked about this concept at
     Willowcreek's 2005 Leadership Summit in his
     message entitled "Action Steps for Monday."